Measure for Measure

as Royal Entertainment

Measure

for Measure

as Royal Entertainment

JOSEPHINE WATERS BENNETT

Columbia University Press
New York & London 1966

Josephine Waters Bennett is Professor of English at Hunter College.

Copyright © 1966 Columbia University Press
Library of Congress Catalog Card Number: 66-15764
Printed in the United States of America

TO THE
FOLGER SHAKESPEARE LIBRARY

Preface

The desire to enlarge life, to expand every area of experience, to find meaning and reward for daily effort takes many directions. Some long to explore the mountains of the moon; for others the exploration of human experience has greater value. This book records an attempt to understand one of Shakespeare's most puzzling plays by placing it, not only in the map of an era, but more definitely within the landscape of a particular year and day. One of the unexpected rewards of this undertaking is a close-up of Shakespeare himself—a self-portrait which throws light on a central area of his personality and activities. By that light we see something new in other plays besides this one, catching a glimpse of the man as he lived and wrote. This immediacy of observation, this self-portrait shows him, not larger than life, nor diminished or faded by distance, but as his contemporaries knew him.

In the long history of our literary heritage the interpretation of the greatest works—the *Iliad*, the Bible, the *Aeneid*—has followed a common pattern. When these books lost their immediacy as records of a culture, of ideas and ideals expressed in action and recorded and interpreted by a poet they became storehouses of familiar quotations and oracles of supernatural wisdom, consulted like the *sortes Vergilianae*, or as Lincoln consulted his Bible; or they became mirrors in which later generations saw their own image. Both of these tendencies have been at work for a long time on the plays of Shakespeare. Indeed, today, when knowledge of the Bible and the great classics is no longer common, Shakespeare remains the only author who can be quoted or alluded to in educated circles with some hope of general recognition. And he is often quoted, out of context, as an unfailing expression of Truth.

The interpretation of the plays in the light of our own preconceptions—the tendency to see ourselves mirrored in the darkened glass—is both more apparent, and, I believe, more deplorable than quotation out of context. The snowstorm of Freudian criticism which struck the plays in the late nineteenth century has largely spent itself, and the economic interpretation which views the plays in the light of what the public demanded, has lost its newness, although it is still a pitfall for the unwary. Our own time has been guilty of finding realism in Shakespeare, when realism was the highest praise, and allegory, symbolism, and abstraction more recently, when these came into favor. Without some knowledge of history the critic can only see himself, can only recognize what he already knows about humanity and art in the plays. The pleasure of recognition of the timelessness of human nature is a great deal, and the dramatic expression of our own thoughts and emotions helps us to understand ourselves, but that is not the whole.

Shakespeare's own age valued history as an extension of experience, a guide to wise action and a warning against folly. It has also great value as companionship and enlargement of the mind in another direction—in the experience of difference as well as of sameness, the process by which we come the better to know ourselves through the understanding of someone else. History, and especially literary history, increases our experience of otherness, and so our tolerance, by abolishing the provincialism of the here and now. It provides a perspective from which to see ourselves, and so gives proportion and significance to the events and aspirations of our own brief day.

By presenting *Measure for Measure* against the background of history, I have attempted to explain the play as it appeared to its first audience, and as its author intended it. If I have helped the reader to see it afresh, and to understand and enjoy it more fully by bringing something of the mentality and preconceptions of England in 1604 to it, instead of, or in addition to, his own, then the writing of a whole book about a single play will be justified.

In such an undertaking it is hard to know where to begin acknowledging debts. The aid offered to a student of Shakespeare is overwhelming in its volume and variety. It would seem that everything sensible has been said, and yet the discovery of a new fact, such as that *Measure for Measure* was performed at Court on December 26, 1604, makes necessary a reconsideration of everything that has been said about the play. However, if we see more than our predecessors did, it is by standing on their shoulders. To four centuries of Shakespeare scholarship I am indebted, and only a small fraction of that debt has been indicated in the text and notes.

This study had its beginning, on paper, as an undertaking to write a twenty-page article for a quatercentenary volume. It quickly outgrew the space allotted, outgrew any space it was reasonable to ask from any learned journal, and left no alternative but to make a small book of it. For encouragement, advice, and helpful criticism I am indebted to Professor James G. McManaway, although he has not yet seen this book. For the opportunity to work at the Folger Shakespeare Library I am indebted to Dr. Louis Bunker Wright, the Director, who awarded me a fellowship which made possible six months of intensive study under the ideal conditions which he has so largely created there. There is no appropriate place to stop acknowledging debts to the staff, but I must surely begin with the Reference Librarian, Dr. Dorothy Mason, who doubles as hostess of the reading room and personal friend to many of its readers. To her I am especially indebted for abundant hospitality which makes every return to the library a homecoming. So many others have contributed both to the efficiency and the amenities of the Folger that I cannot name them all, for I would not be willing to omit anybody. However, I should like to mention Professor Giles Dawson, who is always available for consultation, and who doubles as host at lunch-time. As for the other readers, the Folger is a place to meet old friends, and to make new ones. Its value in this respect only those who have been there can understand.

Finally, I wish to thank my friend and colleague, Professor Babette M. Levy, who advised me on the first chapter and the index, and read the proofs. I must thank also the staff of the Columbia University Press for their help and encouragement— and their patience.

JOSEPHINE WATERS BENNETT

April 25, 1966

Contents

Measure for Measure

as Royal Entertainment

1 · The Problem

A student of the humanities, left hopelessly out of date by revolutionary changes in the sciences in this century, is tempted to comfort himself with the thought that the sciences change and pass, history remains. But in history, as in science, new discoveries make necessary the revision, and even the abandonment of old and long-accepted beliefs. Students of Shakespeare are sometimes overwhelmed with the mass of new facts and theories which the intensive study of every angle of his life and work has produced in this century. The full implications of many of these new facts have not yet been incorporated into the interpretation of his works.

Readers of *Measure for Measure* are familiar with the now discarded theory that it is a "dark comedy" belonging to Shakespeare's "tragic period," a theory which came into the twentieth century in Edward Dowden's famous and scholarly book, *Shakspere: A Critical Study of His Mind and Art,* published in 1874 and in its twelfth edition in 1901. F. S. Boas changed the designation from "dark comedies" to "problem plays" for this group of three plays, *Troilus and Cressida, All's Well that Ends Well,* and *Measure for Measure;*[1] and, while later critics have added to and subtracted from the group, and the notion of a "period of gloom" in the poet's life has been abandoned,[2] *Measure for Measure* has remained a play which "just perplexes and offends, with its deliberate painting of the seamy side of things, through which intolerable personages pass to an end that is certainly determined by no principles of poetic justice. We are in unwholesome company. . . ."[3]

And yet there is evidence, now generally accepted, that this play was chosen, in 1604, for presentation at court to open the Christmas revels, a joyous occasion for which it must have been judged suitable. The evidence is both external and internal, and the latter is overwhelming, but it has been almost entirely overlooked because the external evidence was for a long time suspected of being a forgery. In 1842 Peter Cunningham, a friend and neighbor of John Payne Collier, published *Extracts from the Accounts of the Revels at Court,* mostly from the reign of Queen Elizabeth, but including two for the reign of James I, for the years 1604–5 and 1611–12, the only ones surviving for the later reign.[4] Some twenty-six years later Cunningham tried to sell the original documents to the British Museum, and he accounted for his possession of them by claiming that he had found them in a cellar under Somerset House. They were recovered by the Records Office as official papers, but an official of the British Museum attached a note to the papers throwing doubt on their authenticity. In the 1880s Halliwell-Phillipps pointed out that Edmund Malone, who died before Cunningham was born, had among his papers a memorandum which corresponded very closely to the list of plays published by Cunningham. A controversy ensued which it is not necessary to review here; but in 1923 E. K. Chambers, in his monumental *Elizabethan Stage,* threw the weight of his great authority solidly behind the argument for the authenticity of these two fragments of the Revels Accounts.[5]

This did not end the controversy. In 1928 S. A. Tannenbaum, the American Shakespearean and handwriting expert, undertook to show that the document in question was simply another of J. P. Collier's forgeries;[6] but, in reviewing Tannenbaum's book, W. W. Greg rejected his conclusion, and in 1930 E. K. Chambers reaffirmed his position, in *William Shakespeare: A Study of Facts and Problems*, citing further argument and supporting evidence.[7]

There the matter has rested, and must remain, unless new evidence is discovered, or a new interpretation of existing evidence devised. Tannenbaum was chiefly concerned with the paper, ink, spelling, and handwriting of the documents. Chambers points out the agreement between the disputed Revels Account and the Chamber Accounts. The two agree except in the matter of the payment for *Love's Labour's Lost* which, we know from other sources, was performed during the 1604–5 season, but was not paid for by the King. The list of plays in this Revels Account is a remarkable one, which will be discussed in Chapter VII. Its peculiarity is witness of its authenticity. As an eighteenth- or nineteenth-century forgery it is incredible.

Whatever the origin of the papers in question, there is very good reason to accept the list of plays and dates as authentic, and, having accepted it, we need to explore the implications. As long ago as 1937 R. W. Chambers, in the Annual Shakespeare Lecture before the British Academy, accepting without question the record of a court performance of *Measure for Measure* on December 26, 1604, pointed out that it is a play of forgiveness and reconciliation suitable for the season. He says that Shakespeare remakes the "barbarous old story of *Promos and Cassandra*, removing its morbid details, harmonizing its crudities, giving humanity and humour to its low characters, turning it into a con-

sistent tale of intercession for sin, repentance from and forgiveness of crime." [8]

Unfortunately, this interpretation gave encouragement to the
allegory-hunters, who had already been at work on it, and who
proceeded to interpret it as an allegory, a parable, or a morality
on the theme of forgiveness.[9] This about-face, from seeing the
play as a cynical bit of realism to seeing it as reflecting the Ser-
mon on the Mount, resulted in modification of the "realistic"
view of W. W. Lawrence,[10] with substantial concessions to the
allegorizers. Effort to find a middle ground has resulted in the
conclusion that the play is a technical failure.[11] E. M. W. Tillyard, in his study of Shakespeare's problem plays (1950), finds
something "radically schizophrenic" about it, and, while he rejects
the theory of a "tragic period," he thinks that the poet was in a
"mood of uncommon abstraction and speculation. The themes of
mercy and forgiveness are treated in all sincerity with no shadow
of satire," and therefore "any failure" of the play "is not of
morale but of technique." [12] He finds this failure in the highly
contrived fifth act and traces it back to the point in Act III where
the Duke takes control of the situation and begins to manipulate
events.[13]

The most recent study, *The Problem Plays of Shakespeare,*
by Ernest Schanzer, still clings to the notion that the play is
realistic at base. He defines the problem play as "a play in which
we find a concern with a moral problem which is central to it,
presented in such a manner that we are unsure of our moral
bearings, so that uncertain and divided responses to it in the
minds of the audience are possible or even probable." [14] This defi-
nition may fit a modern problem play, but it seems improbable
that Shakespeare intended any such effect. As Alfred Harbage
has pointed out, much of the playwright's success results from

the firmness of his grasp of, and response to, the morality of his day.[15]

The preconception with which critics continue to approach the play is still that created by the discovery that *Measure for Measure* was written between tragedies, and this preconception creates a primary concern with character. From Coleridge to Schanzer every discussion of the play begins with analysis of the characters, whereas the basis of comedy, even more certainly than of tragedy, is plot.[16] Shakespeare usually takes an old story and provides it with characters so suited to the action that, if we did not know the source, we might easily imagine that the characters had given rise to the action. Since we know the source of the plot, we must see that the question Shakespeare asked himself was, what kind of people would behave in this way? not, what would these people do in these circumstances? The result is a firmness of character delineation which gives life and credibility to the most fantastic plots. In tragedy the characters must be fully developed, so that the action may seem natural and inevitable, that is, may *seem* to grow out of character. In comedy the characters are more lightly sketched, more typical, more obviously the product of the plot. Therefore, analysis of comedy which begins with character simply begs the question.

It is the plot which determines whether a play shall be tragic or comic, and the characters are created accordingly. Hermia's problem, in *A Midsummer Night's Dream,* is the same as Juliet's, but the actions, the characters, and the solutions of this problem are as different as comedy and tragedy can make them. Even more striking is the contrast between Othello and Leontes. For both the problem is "real" in that the consequences of their jealousy are dire, yet Shakespeare, adapting character to plot, gave Othello our sympathy and full understanding by every device available to him, while he carefully omitted every detail of the old story which justified or made reasonable Leontes' behavior. In one play he was creating, that is, interpreting, a tragic character for whom he must arouse the audience's sympathy, in the other he was telling a winter's tale in which, not Leontes, but the consequences of his irrational and absurd jealousy are central. In *Much Ado About Nothing* jealousy is dealt with even more lightly. Hero is "dead" for a few days, Hermione for a generation, Desdemona forever. It is not the seriousness of the "real life" dilemma, but the artist's treatment of it, which determines whether the play is "realistic" or not.

Measure for Measure presents, if not a "true to life," at least a dire, situation. Claudio is about to be beheaded for seducing his intended, and his sister Isabella is given a choice between her brother's life and her chastity. Moreover, Shakespeare has provided this play, like *Much Ado About Nothing* and most of his other comedies, with "realistic," or low-life, contrast in the persons of Mistress Overdone, her bawd Pompey, and her customers, Lucio and Froth. This group while it can hardly be said to constitute an underplot, effectively creates the atmosphere of moral corruption and its punishment which serves as setting for Claudio's indiscretion.

This low-life material has been variously and curiously treated; on the one hand its prominence in the play has been enormously exaggerated, and on the other its function in the plot has been largely ignored. Two versions of the play produced in the Restoration and during the eighteenth century omitted it altogether, substituting other matter.[17] Even Garrick cut these parts severely, and Kemble followed Garrick's example. Samuel Johnson seems to have been almost alone in finding the "light or comick part . . . very natural and pleasing," although he did not admire the play as a whole.[18] A famous modern critic describes it as "a comedy only in the technical sense that it concludes with the chief characters still alive; its somber prison scenes, its grotesque and hideous figure of Abhorson, the executioner, and Barnardine, the condemned desperado, its magnificent speeches in contempt of life and in terror of death, its sinister hypocrite Angelo, and its riff-raff of bawds, beadles, and fribbles, all stamp it as from the tragic mint." [19]

Can this be the play selected for the entertainment of King James and his court at the beginning of a Christmas season? The only record of a performance of *Measure for Measure* in Shakespeare's lifetime is that in the Revels Accounts discovered by Cunningham. If we accept this record as genuine, then this was the play selected by the Lord Chamberlain and his deputy, the Master of the Revels, in consultation with the King's Men, to open the festivities of the twelve days of Christmas on the occasion when King James spent the holiday at Whitehall for the first time. Although King James was celebrating his second Christmas in England, this was the first for which extensive preparations could be made. He had arrived in London in May, 1603, at the beginning of an especially violent and prolonged outbreak of the plague.[20] The theaters, closed March 19 in anticipation of the death of Queen Elizabeth (who died on the 24th), were not reopened for over a year.[21]

Shakespeare's company toured during the summer and seems to have stayed out of London. The players were at Mortlake in Surrey on December 2, 1603, when they went from Mortlake to Wilton to amuse the King with a play.[22] On December 12 the King went to Hampton Court, well outside the urban area, to keep Christmas. Shakespeare's company, now the King's Men, was paid for six plays acted between December 26 and January 6, and for two more presented on February 2 and 19,[23] but the public theaters did not reopen until after April 9, 1604. We do not know the names of several plays acted during that first Christmas season but, with so much uncertainty, so little time and place to prepare, and so many plays in their repertory which the King and Queen had not seen, it seems inevitable that these plays were selected from the existing repertory of the company.

The second Christmas was a very different matter. As we would expect, the Christmas revels of 1604–5 were abundantly prepared for and prolonged. Dudley Carleton wrote to John Chamberlain on January 15, "It seems we shall have Christmas all the year." [24] Twelfth Night usually ended the "season," but in 1604–5 there were plays on January 7 and 8.[25] Then the King went hunting to Royston, and the Queen and most of the Court were entertained by the Earl of Southampton with a play, and by Robert Cecil, now Lord Cranborne, perhaps also with a play. In addition, "The Temples have both of them done somewhat since Twelftide." [26]

If, as the first play of this gala season, *Measure for Measure* was selected, that is a primary fact which must be taken into account in any attempt to interpret the play as its author intended it, and as its contemporary audience understood it. It must be seen, not as a play written between *Othello* and *Macbeth*, or *King Lear*, but as a play selected for the entertainment of the new King and his court on a very important and joyous occasion. It was selected to open the celebration of the Christmas season of 1604–5, and there is much evidence in the text of the play to indicate that it was planned and written for that season, as will appear in due course.

It is, as R. W. Chambers pointed out, a tale of repentance and forgiveness, and as such, it would be suitable for the Christmas revels. But, in addition to the basic plot, it contains much topical matter which indicates that it was written expressly for King James, and for this particular occasion. Two topical allusions, the second hitherto unidentified, refer it specifically to this Christmas and confirm the record in the Revels Accounts that it was seen by King James and his court at this time. It contains an allusion, as John Dover Wilson observed, to Ben Jonson's *Masque of Blackness,* which was scheduled for performance on Twelfth Night, that is, twelve days later.[27] Dr. Wilson weakens his case by assuming that the preparations for this, the first of Jonson's elaborate masks, were secret. On the contrary, the extravagant cost of the machines provided by Inigo Jones was a subject of gossip early in December,[28] and the fact that the Queen and eleven of her ladies were preparing to take part in it not only made secrecy impossible, but gave rise to much gossip and some censure.[29] It was a great novelty, eagerly looked forward to. Shakespeare makes Angelo say:

> Thus wisdom wishes to appear most bright
> When it doth tax itself, as these black masks
> Proclaim an enshield beauty ten times louder
> Than beauty could, displayed.   (II, iv, 78–81)[30]

This is a graceful compliment to the "wisdom" and beauty of the Queen, who had requested a mask of blackamoors;[31] and the audience could be trusted to catch the reference.

There is a second topical allusion at the opening of I, ii:

Lucio. If the Duke, with the other dukes, come not to composition with the king of Hungary, why then all the dukes fall upon the king.

1 Gentleman. Heaven grant us its peace, but not the king of Hungary's!

The key to this matter, hitherto unnoticed,[32] is provided by John Chamberlain, who wrote from the court on December 10, 1604, "The Duke of Holst is here still procuring a levie of men to carie into Hungarie." [33] The Duke of Holst, or Holstein, was Queen Anne's brother Ulrich, who came to court before November 14, and stayed until June 1.[34] It would be difficult to discover what he planned, since nothing came of it, but Hungary was at this time partitioned between the Turks and the Empire, and the two were at war from 1593 to 1606. Meanwhile the emperor, Rudolph II, undertook to suppress Protestantism in Transylvania, and in 1602–4 one of his generals, Stephen Bocskay, a Hungarian Protestant, led a revolt against the Catholic reaction, and in October, 1604, won a decisive victory at the battle of Adrion, and set about to secure (with the aid of the Turkish Porte) religious liberty in Transylvania and Hungary. The Porte invested him with the Voivodship of Transylvania and Kingdom of Hungary in 1604; he was confirmed king by the Hungarian Diet in 1605, and negotiated the treaty of Vienna and the peace of Zsitva-Torok in 1606. Bocskay and his followers found the Turk more tolerant than the Catholic reaction, but how the Protestant princes in the West viewed the situation is another matter. In 1602 Henri IV had refused to aid the emperor against the Turks. An attempt to rally the German Protestant archdukes against the emperor may be the basis of Lucio's reference to "the Duke and the other dukes." At any rate, in 1604, the king of Hungary's peace would be a victory for the Turks and a defeat for Christendom.[35] But any peace would be undesirable to a band of adventurers such as the Duke of Holst was recruiting. Chamberlain goes on to say, "but me thinckes they should have litle to do that wold adventure themselves so far with a man able to do them no more goode." Lucio's reference to "the Duke" and "the

other dukes" is, of course, primarily a reference to the Duke of
Vienna in the play, but it also glances with polite ambiguity at
the Duke of Holst in the audience and to the general political
situation. The choice of Vienna as the locale of the play may also
reflect current interest.

Two allusions can, of course, be inserted into an already completed play, but there are many structural features of this play
which show that it was planned and written for a Christmas
entertainment for King James early in his reign, and these two
topical references identify for us the particular Christmas in question. Major elements in the plot show that the part of the Duke is
modeled on the King's own account of his principles of government,[36] Angelo's behavior agrees with the conduct attributed by
King James to a tyrant; Lucio, a character not in the source plot,
in addition to connecting the underplot with the main plot, provides a comic representation of the type of person who libels his
ruler as King James complained of being libeled.

We must not forget, in our emphasis on the public theater as
the chief formative influence on Shakespeare's art, that a major
part of the players' excuse for their profession was the duty of
providing entertainment for the monarch. In 1604 Shakespeare's
company enjoyed royal patronage. The players had had a sub-
sidy and other favors. If they did not have a new play ready and
suitable for the Christmas revels at court, they were remiss in
their duty; and if their chief playwright did not produce a
comedy especially for the occasion, he must have been in a very
dark mood indeed. But there was a new comedy.

The idea that this play, or at least the first half of it, is "realistic" arises partly from its creation of believable characters, and
partly from its theme, the administration of justice, designed to
interest King James, who prided himself on his "kingcraft." The

earlier comedies reflect the atmosphere of Queen Elizabeth's
court and, anticipating performance before her, were concerned
with the affairs of lovers. Queen Elizabeth made courtship the
convention both of her diplomacy and of her government. The
abrupt change in the convention of courtiership which marked
the accession of King James is strikingly illustrated in the literature of the period. It can be seen very simply by comparing
Measure for Measure with *A Midsummer Night's Dream.*

The latter takes us immediately into the storybook world of
Theseus and Hippolyta and is concerned with courtship and the
vicissitudes of lovers, while the former creates its storybook world
with no more magic than a mysterious Duke who goes into hiding in order to watch his deputy administer a preposterous "law
of Vienna," which it is equally reprehensible to enforce or not to
enforce. On this slender basis Shakespeare has erected a swift-
moving and highly theatrical comedy. Surely we must ask, if
this is a play which must be taken seriously because it deals
"seriously with the problems of life," [37] just what are these problems? Is Isabella's predicament, forced to choose between her
brother's life and her chastity, any more a real-life problem than
Hermia's, forced to choose between an unwanted husband and
a nunnery? And does she really make a choice? Or is she rather,
caught on the horns of a dilemma and rescued by the Duke?

Shakespeare has so successfully created the *illusion* of reality
that he has misled his critics, casting the spell of the theater over
a plot deliberately exaggerated into absurdity. He has taken the
old folk tale of a woman (sometimes a wife and sometimes a
sister) who must sacrifice her chastity to save her husband, or
brother,[38] and has converted it to his own purpose. He knew
the story in one of Whetstone's versions, where it was well on the
way, through the shaping power of the imagination, to as pure

fiction as anything in the brothers Grimm. And in Shakespeare's
capable hands it lost the last trace of real-life cruelty and injustice.

We need to examine this play with fresh eyes, and in the light
of the gala occasion for which it was chosen, and even written,
putting out of our minds all that has been said about it, so that
we can read the text, which is a very good one as texts of Shakespeare's plays go,[39] with completely open minds. So viewed on the
stage of our imaginations, it becomes a new and very different
play from the one which has been misunderstood for so long.
And this fresh view will give us also an exciting glimpse of the
poet-actor at work, one which will shed light on other plays as
well.

11 · The Plot

Where the source of his plot is known, one of the surest guides to Shakespeare's intention is observation of his manipulation of his materials. The source or sources of the plot of *Measure for Measure* have been exhaustively and repeatedly studied,[1] but too much attention has been paid to his borrowings, too little to the manipulations and mutations which show his intention. The story, like that of *Othello* (produced in the same year), came directly or indirectly from Giraldi Cintio's *Ecatommiti,* a collection of tales first published in 1565 and 1566. Cintio made the story into a tragicomedy which he called *Epitia* and published in 1583. Meanwhile, George Whetstone turned it into a pair of tragicomedies which he published as *The Right Excellent and famous Historye, of Promos and Cassandra,* in 1578. They seem never to have been acted,[2] but in 1582 he retold his version of the tale in his *Heptameron of Civill Discourses,* a work which was reprinted in 1593 as *Aurelia, the Paragon of Pleasure and Princely Delights.* In France, Claude Rouillet used a similar plot for his Latin tragedy, *Philanira,* published in 1556. This play was republished in French in 1563 and 1577, and Whetstone probably used it.[3] Cintio's *Ecatommiti* was translated into French by Gabriel Chappuy in 1584, and there are several other versions of the story which Shakespeare could have read,[4] but it seems highly improbable that he borrowed as many details from as many sources as the sum total of alleged borrowings would amount to. In 1604 Shakespeare did not need Whetstone's play to suggest to him a realistic, low-life underplot to complement the main plot, nor Cintio's play to provide material for a discussion of "justice and mercy and the duty of judges,"[5] to say nothing of lesser details such as the name "Angelo" (in *Epitia* the sister of the condemned man is Angela). As we shall see, Shakespeare's comic underplot owes much to his own earlier comedies and nothing to Whetstone, and his theme of justice and mercy derives from a different source altogether.

Actually, Whetstone's retelling of his version, in the *Heptameron,* juxtaposes the three main elements of Shakespeare's plot, and these are not found together in any of the other analogues. It is described on its title page as "The Christmas Exercise of sundrie well courted Gentlemen and Gentlewomen," and the story of Promos and Cassandra is told as a reply to a tale of the "bed-trick." The fictional framework of the *Heptameron* represents the author as arriving at a castle in Italy on Christmas eve and being entertained there. The Lady Aurelia is selected as queen of the Christmas pleasures and the topic selected for discussion is "the honorable institution of marriage." On the fourth day one of the men tells a tale of "The Adventure of Fryer *Inganno,*" which, while it bears no resemblance to Shakespeare's plot, involves a humorous version of the "bed-trick." The Friar is hoaxed by having an old hag substituted for the simple wife with whom he has made an assignation, and he is hazed further by the village priest and his cohorts. As an answer to this tale, one of the ladies (curiously enough her name is Isabella) tells the story of Promos and Cassandra. Here, together, are the Christmas occasion, the bed-trick, and the story of the monstrous ran-som. If Shakespeare was thinking of writing a comedy for the Christmas entertainment of the court, he might well have turned through this attractive little book and found all that he actually took from the old plot. The story begins:

At what time *Corvinus* the scourge of the *Turkes,* rayned as Kinge of Bohemia: for to well governe the free Cities of his Realme, he sent divers worthy Maierstrates. Among the rest, he gave the Lorde *Promos* the Lieutennauntship of *Iulio*: who in the beginning of his government, purged the Cittie of many ancient vices, and severely punished new offenders.

In this Cittie there was an olde custome (by the suffering of some maiestrates growne out of use) that what man so ever com-mitted Adulterie should lose his head: And the woman offender should ever after be infamously noted, by the wearing of some disguised apparrell: For the man was held to bee the greatest offender, and therefore had the severest punishment.

Lord *Promos,* with a rough execution, revived this Statute, and in the hyest degree of injurie, brake it hymselfe, as shall appeare by the sequell of *Andrugioes* adventures.

This *Andrugio,* by the yeelding favor of fayre *Polina,* trespassed against the ordinance, who, through envie, was accused, and by Lorde *Promos,* condemned to suffer execution.

The woefull *Cassandra, Andrugio's* Sister, prostrates herself at Lord *Promos* feete, and with more teares than wordes, thus pleaded for her Brothers Lyfe . . . (sig. Nii^v).

This is the story line, which Shakespeare filled out in his own way, combining the tale of the monstrous ransom with his own version of the bed-trick used in *All's Well that Ends Well,* and giving the whole a meaning suitable to the occasion and the audi-ence for which he was writing.

Whether it was Whetstone's play or his Christmas story which Shakespeare had in mind, Whetstone was his immediate source; but we are guided to his intention, not by the similarities of detail, but by the major changes in plot and characterization which he made. Cintio's story, which he probably knew, is a brutal tale. A man is sentenced to be beheaded for rape. His sister, Epitia, appeals to the governor, Juriste, for mercy. He offers to pardon her brother if she will yield to his lust. She reluctantly consents, is deflowered, and then Juriste sends her the decapitated body of her brother. She appeals to the emperor, who forces Juriste to marry her and then orders his execution. Epitia, now Juriste's wife, intercedes for him and he is pardoned. Whetstone renames the characters and softens the plot considerably by reducing the brother's crime from rape to the seduction of a sweetheart whom he is willing to marry. Then he saves the young man's life by having the jailor (very secretly) arrange his escape in disguise and decapitate another prisoner (who is already dead) in his place. However, he allows the sister, Cassandra, to pay the monstrous ransom. The first of the two plays ends with Cassandra's announcement that she has buried her brother (as she supposes) and will go and complain to the king and then kill herself. In the second part, Promos, the wicked governor, is forced by the king to marry her, and then, just as he is to be executed for murdering her brother, Andrugio (conveniently present) throws off his disguise and saves Promos' life at the risk of his own, since he is still under sentence.

In the process of softening the crude injustices of the old plot, Whetstone has created a melodramatic absurdity which probably amused Shakespeare, for he further increased the disproportion between the punishment and the crime. Beheading, as punishment for the seduction of a sweetheart whom the seducer is willing to marry was, and is, preposterous;[6] but Shakespeare made the old "law of Vienna" even more absurd by representing that the binding part of the marriage vows had already been exchanged. Claudio's intention is honorable. He and Julietta have exchanged vows privately, and in the second scene he says before witnesses, "She is fast my wife," "upon a true contract." [7] Only the public ceremony has been delayed because of a dowry, "remaining in the coffer of her friends" (I, ii, 146). This was a rather common situation in Shakespeare's England.[8] If it was not the poet's own situation when he married,[9] it was certainly that of his good friend, Thomas Russell, who lived with the widow, Anne Digges, for three years before they could clear her dowry and solemnize the marriage. This they did on August 26, 1603, a year before *Measure for Measure* was written.[10]

Beheading was a punishment reserved in England for traitors of noble blood or great political importance. The punishment of men for sexual immorality was rare and mild. Baker's *Chronicle* reports a case occurring about this time which throws light on what Shakespeare's audience could be expected to think of the "law of Vienna" which condemned Claudio to be beheaded for getting his betrothed wife with child. Baker reports, "On Sunday the 24. of *October,* an exemplar pennance was imposed upon Sir *Pecksall Brockas* Knight, which was to stand at *Pauls* Crosse in a white sheet, holding a stick in his hand, having been formerly convicted before the high Commissioners, for many notorious Adulteries with divers women." [11] Comparison of this sentence with the fantastic savagery of Claudio's gives us a measure of the "realism" of the play.

A somewhat sterner view was taken of the activities of professionals, like Mistress Overdone and Pompey, her bawd, as we can see from an entry in the diary of William Fleetwood, Re-

corder of London, for anuary, 1582–3: "Vpon monday m^r·
Smithe m^r· Owen and my selff occupied all the days wth m^r
deane [i.e., the Dean] in westm' for the punishm^t of bawdes &
strompetz of whom some were whipped, some were carted, but all
banished." [12] Shakespeare has not only increased the disproportion between the crime and its punishment by minimizing Claudio's crime, but he has further emphasized its severity by providing a realistic background of professional vice and *its* punishment.

In the light of the everyday morality of the time, the "law of
Vienna" appears as a comic device which, like the beanstalk in
the fairy tale, removes the story from reality by its palpable absurdity. The talk of beheading is to be taken no more seriously
in *Measure for Measure* than it is in *The Mikado*. Indeed, if we
take it seriously we put ourselves in the position of the old coun-
trywoman who said of *The Mikado* that all that talk about cut-
ting off people's heads made her nervous. Shakespeare makes use
of several devices for removing his scene from reality, but by the
beginning of the nineteenth century the perspective of his play
had been lost, and it became possible to regard Claudio's predicament as a "real" one and Isabella's dilemma as a "real-life
problem." Acting and audience are an integral part of any play,
and we must recover something of the mentality of the original
audience if we are to get our bearings and keep our directions
straight.

In addition to this exaggeration of the disproportion between
Claudio's crime and its punishment, Shakespeare also exaggerates
the purity of Isabella and the moral rectitude and inexperience of
Angelo. Cintio and Whetstone both make the sister a virgin, but
Shakespeare makes her a wide-eyed innocent who is just about
to enter the strictest order of nuns she can find and "wishing a
more strict restraint/upon the sisterhood." The governor of the

city in both Cintio and Whetstone is experienced, but Angelo is
young and inexperienced in either government or sex; and this
youthful inexperience tends to extenuate both his severity and his
villainy. He protests his appointment as the Duke's deputy, saying:

> Let there be some more test made of my mettle
> Before so noble and so great a figure
> Be stamped upon it.   (I, i, 47–49)

The Duke describes him as "A man of stricture and firm ab-
stinence" (I, iii, 12). Later he says:

> Lord Angelo is precise,
> Stands at a guard with envy; scarce confesses
> That his blood flows, or that his appetite
> Is more to bread than stone.   (I, iii, 50–53)

In his youth and ignorance of his own potentialities, Angelo is
overconfident and self-righteous. He tells Escalus:

> You may not so extenuate his [Claudio's] offense
> For [i.e., because] I have had such faults; but rather tell me,
> When I that censure him do so offend,
> Let mine own judgment pattern out my death . . . (II, i, 27–30)

At the end of the next scene, after his first interview with Isabella, when he confesses his temptation in soliloquy, he reveals
his self-righteousness again, saying,

> O cunning enemy that, to catch a saint,
> With saints dost bait thy hook; . . .   (II, 180–81)

and

> Never could the strumpet
> With all her double vigor, art and nature,

> Once stir my temper; but this virtuous maid
> Subdues me quite. Ever till now
> When men were fond, I smiled and wondered how.
>
> (ll. 183–87)

Angelo's sudden discovery of sex appetite is credible, and even forgivable,[13] if we allow him youth and inexperience. Shakespeare makes clear his uneasy conscience (II, ii, 161–87; II, iv, 1–17; and IV, iv, 18–32), and so prepares the way for his repentance and forgiveness.

The two basic changes by which Shakespeare converts the old melodrama into comedy are the change in the decision of Isabella and the enlargement of the part of the Duke. Isabella never for a moment considers ransoming her brother at the price of her virginity. She has no dilemma, faces no serious problem,[14] she is simply outraged. And she also is self-righteous, as only a young and inexperienced girl can be, without being an offensive prude.

This change in the part of Isabella made necessary the extension of the part of the Duke. Cintio brings in the emperor, at the end of his story, as the overlord who punishes an unjust governor. Whetstone merely changes the identity of this superior power to "Corvinus the scourge of the Turkes . . . Kinge of Bohemia." Shakespeare reduces his rank, but makes him the *deus ex machina* of the whole play. Like Prospero, Duke Vincentio creates the situation and then resolves it, using disguise instead of magic to achieve his ends.

In the first act the Duke creates the situation by abdicating, states his purpose to test Angelo, and announces his intention to remain in Vienna disguised as a friar to watch him. And then, when Angelo proposes the monstrous ransom, and Isabella (true to herself, but contrary to the old plot) has refused to save her brother's life at that price, the Duke-disguised-as-a-friar steps in, produces Mariana, like a rabbit out of a hat, and arranges that she should substitute for Isabella and so save Claudio. Then, when Angelo (true to the old plot) breaks his word and orders the prompt execution, instead of the pardon, of Claudio, the Duke-Friar is again hard put to it to save Claudio. He proposes the substitution of Barnardine, who is also under sentence of death; but Barnardine firmly refuses to be executed that day, and so the kind jailor suggests the substitution of the head of Ragozine, "a most notorious pirate . . . who died this morning" (IV, iii, 66–73). "O, 'tis an accident that heaven provides," exclaims the Duke-Friar. In order to persuade the Provost to disobey Angelo's order, the Friar (Duke) has to promise the Duke's return, and so he proceeds to "return"; and, by elaborate play-acting, in which he is forced to coach several assistants, and to tell several lies, he brings Angelo to repentance, putting him in Claudio's place. He also brings Isabella to a state of Christian charity in which she begs forgiveness for her enemy, and so redeems herself, fulfilling the condition of the Lord's Prayer, "Forgive us our sins as we forgive those who sin against us."

The play is "highly artificial and contrived" not merely from the middle of Act III, but from the beginning. When, in the third scene of Act I, the Duke discloses that he plans to stay in Vienna disguised as a Friar, to watch Angelo, Shakespeare is reassuring his audience that this is to be a comedy. That is the function of the scene. The first act gets the play under way with Shakespeare's usual deftness and dispatch. In scene i, the Duke of Vienna announces that he is going on a journey and leaving the experienced administrator, Escalus, and the young and inexperienced Angelo, to rule in his place. Angelo is to have absolute power: "Mortality and mercy in Vienna/ Live in thy tongue and heart" (ll. 44–45). Scene ii introduces Mistress Overdone

and her customers, and we learn that Angelo's first act has been
to revive the old "law of Vienna," and that Claudio is to be its
first victim. Scene iii immediately reassures the audience: the
Duke is not going away at all, he will stay and watch Angelo.
This scene (54 lines) is entirely devoted to the Duke's explanation to Friar Thomas of just why he has appointed Angelo in his
place and wishes to disguise himself so that he can remain in
Vienna and see whether Angelo is what he seems, or "If power
change purpose, what our seemers be." In other words, the Duke's
purpose is to test Angelo by giving him absolute power and seeing how he uses it.

His disguise is a comic device, not a preparation for either
realism or tragedy. Scene iv, the last scene in the act, introduces
Isabella and sets her on her way to Angelo to plead for her
brother's life. This is too tight and economical a first act to allow
us to suppose that scene iii is of less than major importance in
the construction of the play. Moreover, while Act II opens with a
scene showing Angelo's lack of capacity as a governor, and two
of the other three scenes of this act are devoted to developing
the conflict between Isabella and Angelo, nevertheless, Shakespeare does not allow his audience to forget that the Duke is in
Vienna and watching. Scene iii shows him catechising Julietta,
an action which has no consequences in the plot, but which
establishes the Duke's presence (in his disguise as a Friar), his
sound morality, and his full knowledge of Claudio's situation. It
prepares the audience also for the opening of Act III, where his
"consolation" of Claudio keeps him firmly on the scene at the
critical moment.

This moment comes in the middle of Act III, when Isabella,
having failed to save Claudio, fails also in charity towards him.
The Duke-Friar comes forward and takes control of the situation.

However, since he is in disguise, Shakespeare twice reminds the audience that the Friar is really the Duke. At the end of Act III he speaks a soliloquy, not as a friar but as the Duke meditating on the duty of a governor. Again, in the first scene of Act IV, when Isabella has taken Mariana aside to instruct her how to find her way to Angelo's bed, the Friar speaks a soliloquy of "place and greatness" which identifies him as the Duke. Thereafter, throughout the six short scenes which make up Act IV, there is no need for further reminders. The Friar's first scheme to save Claudio proves a failure in scene ii, and he is forced to produce a letter from the Duke. The whole humor of the situation depends on the fact that the Friar *is* the Duke but cannot admit it. In order to persuade the honest Provost to disobey Angelo's order, he is forced to promise that the Duke will return within two days. Thereafter he is busy preparing for that "return" and his pretenses are amusing because they are pretenses. In Act V he has returned.

Too much attention to the "source" has, in this case, obscured the act of genius by which Shakespeare has metamorphosed his materials into comedy. By solemnly accepting the situation in Act I as "realistic," and overlooking the significance of the Duke's continuing presence in Vienna, modern critics have postponed the recognition of the artificial elements in this play until the middle of Act III, and so have broken the play in two. *Measure for Measure* is comedy throughout, not only in the artificial plot, exaggerated into absurdity, but in its speeches and situations as well. The difference between a comic and a tragic plot is surely that in comedy the threatened catastrophe can always be averted by explanation or human intervention, whereas in tragedy it arises out of acts that are irreversible. Shakespeare's recognition of this distinction is patent in his fondness for disguises and mistaken identity in comic plots. In this play the good Duke is present in disguise throughout, so that no injustice can be done.

By arranging to spare both Isabella and Claudio, he has turned Whetstone's melodrama into comedy. With his usual economy of invention, he has saved Isabella by creating Mariana and making use of the bed-trick. He has saved Claudio, as Whetstone did, by using a kind jailer and a substitute head, but he has doubled the supply of heads by creating Barnardine, the hardened criminal sentenced to die on the same day as Claudio, and then sparing his in favor of that of Ragozine who (as in Whetstone's version) is already dead. And so there is no harm done, neither rape nor execution, outrageous or deserved, to mar the happy ending.

The absurdity of the "law of Vienna," whose injustice is repeatedly indicated, by the protests not only of Claudio, Lucio, Mistress Overdone, and Pompey, but also of the just Escalus and the honest Provost, puts the sympathies of the audience so fully on the side of Claudio that his execution is as unthinkable as Nanki-Poo's. The jokes about beheading, beginning in the second scene when Claudio is being led to prison and states his case, continuing through Lucio's protests and Pompey's witty remarks, and rising to Barnardine's "I will not consent to die this day, that's certain," these too are reassurances to the audience that this is a comedy.

It is excellent theater, expertly contrived, full of poetry, yet of poetry kept within the confines of rhetoric, never allowed to soar into tragic intensity. There is, however, as R. W. Chambers perceived,[15] a clearly intended, playfully suggested, yet serious core of meaning for the wiser sort's after-meditation. Unfortunately, Chambers was too much involved with his quixotic defense of

Isabella to see more of this meaning than the sin of Angelo, its repentance and forgiveness. There is much more than that. There is clear and repeated allusion to the occasion—to the meaning of Christmas.

This is not to say that the play is an allegory. The method of allegory is to personify ideal concepts and set them to acting in ways typical and illustrative of the concept they represent. The whole art of allegory lies in the delicate balance by which the personification suggests the idea, and the idea the person. The personification must never degenerate into a mere human being. Una must never cease to be Una and become merely a girl in love; and Redcrosse, however human his failings, must never develop such idiosyncrasies of character or action that he ceases to be a universal image of Man and becomes a mere individual. Shakespeare's method is at the opposite pole from allegory. He begins with human beings, and whatever ideal significance they may suggest on reflection, they remain human beings.

Measure for Measure follows the archetypal pattern of the fall and redemption of man, but follows it as Goldsmith followed the story of Job in *The Vicar of Wakefield,* not as MacLeish followed it in *J.B.*[16] The innocence of Isabella and of Angelo, their untried self-confidence, their failure, and their redemption by a superior benevolence echo the pattern of the fall of man and his redemption through God's grace. Isabella tempts Angelo, though not in the way Eve tempted Adam, and Angelo falls and goes on to the sin of Cain in his order for the execution of Claudio; and then the Duke-Friar steps in and the reign of mercy begins.

There are several hints that this parallel was fully intended, that *Measure for Measure* was written with a view to the Christ-

mas performance of which we have record. Isabella, in her plea
for Claudio's life, says,

> Why, all the souls that were were forfeit once,
> And He that might the vantage best have took,
> Found out the remedy.   (II, ii, 73–75)

The Friar, in the speech in which he promises the return of the
Duke, utters a poetic and richly ambiguous line of poetry which
stands out in the text because the rest of the speech is plain prose;
he says, "Look, th'unfolding star calls up the shepherd" (IV, ii,
194–95). The court audience had celebrated Christmas morning
just the day before, and would surely be reminded of the star
and the shepherds of the Nativity story.[17] The promise of the
Duke's return implies the return of justice with mercy, since he
is the rightful ruler and his merciful character has been established in the first act of the play. In the final scene Isabella is
invited by the Duke to invoke the Old Testament law of retribu-
tive justice (V, i, 403–5) but she chooses instead to act in the
spirit of the new law of mercy, and so her sins are washed away
by her plea for the forgiveness of her enemy. Angelo directly
recognizes the power of God in his earthly representative,

> When I perceive your grace, like power divine,
> Hath looked upon my passes . . .   (V, i, 365–66)

In this frame of reference the "law of Vienna" falls into its
ironic place, since the wages of sin is death. And this larger meaning fully justifies the forgiveness of Angelo which so outraged
Coleridge's sense of poetic justice. The prison, in which so many
of the scenes take place, was a well-worn trope for this world.
The question has been asked, why is Barnardine in the play?[18]

And why is he spared? Barnardine is the lost sheep, evidence and symbol of the ultimate extent of the Divine mercy.

In this Christmas context, the pervasive concern of the play with sex becomes appropriate.[19] While sex was not regarded as the cause of the fall of man, it was the result. Man, no longer immortal, was provided with a means of self-perpetuation through generation. As King James put it, echoing the Prayer Book of Edward VI, marriage was ordained "for staying of lust, for procreation of children; & that man should by his wife get a helper like himselfe." [20] The concern of the play with sex is therefore appropriate as well as useful, and it had a delicately humorous bearing on that first Christmas performance. It was written to be presented before King James who made great claim to chastity and invited comparison with Queen Elizabeth in this respect.[21] On the other hand, the Queen was known to be pregnant (she gave birth in April),[22] so that the author was safe from any possible suspicion that the play's discussion of justice and mercy as applied to sex could have any topical significance for the King. He was neither in Claudio's nor in Angelo's position, neither too hot nor too cold, but safely and dutifully married.

Sex, in all its aspects, was proper to the larger meaning of the play, where the institution of marriage and the procreation of children is not only the human condition, in man's fallen state, but is also, paradoxically, the instrument of man's redemption.[23] I have pointed out that in Whetstone's *Heptameron* the topic chosen for seven days' discussion was "a civill contention" of marriage versus a single life (sig. C2^v), in which the debate is decided in favor of marriage. This is not to say that Shakespeare must have taken the idea from Whetstone. He was, I believe, capable of thinking of it for himself, but Whetstone's use of the theme is an indication of how appropriate to the celebration of

the Nativity the discussion of marriage seemed to the Elizabethans. Christmas is not "the atonement" [24] but the manifestation
of divine benevolence which gives promise of salvation through
forgiveness; it is the rainbow and the star, not the crown and the
cross. In the spirit of the season this is a Christmas play, and its
deeper significance would not be wasted on King James, who
prided himself on his theological learning and was much concerned with religion as part of the duty (and power) of divinely
appointed kings. Early in his reign, in January, 1604, he had
called the Hampton Court Conference to establish greater con-
formity in religion, and he took such an active part in the discussion, as the champion of episcopacy, that Archbishop Whit-
gift thought "that the King spake by the Spirit of God." [25]

Measure for Measure is, in a sense, a nativity play, but a highly
sophisticated one. The touch is light and playful, full of paradox
and theatricality, witty, short, and fast-moving—as King James
liked his entertainment. It is a very masculine play, full of masculine humor, yet with an after-image worthy of the meditation
of the most serious. It is small wonder that this play was chosen
by the authorities for the purpose for which it had been written,
to open the Christmas Revels at court in 1604.

III · The Pleasure of Art

Measure for Measure is not only artfully contrived comedy throughout, but the art and artifice are made so obvious that they have troubled critics who tried to see it as a cynical bit of realism. Shakespeare has taken a tragicomic plot and not only removed all elements of tragedy from it, but has treated the resulting comedy with unusually patent showmanship, as if it were an exhibition piece. Mockery is, of course, inherent in paradox, and this play, whether on the ostensible or the archetypal level, is based on paradox. Its mockery is not derisive, however; it is the mockery of imitation—of simulation, by which we are aware simultaneously of opposites, of both sides of a truth, of both reality and pretense. Just as stage disguises require for their enjoyment that the audience be aware simultaneously of the "real" and the pretended character of Viola or Rosalind, so in this play we are kept constantly aware of the *acting* even while we are held in suspense by the *story*.

This staginess is not illusion, not the art which conceals art, but the art which we enjoy for its own sake, the art of virtuosity. The play not only gives us the disguised and highly dramatic Duke, but it is arranged so that each of the major characters, first Isabella, then Angelo, then Claudio, and finally the Duke has a

"big" scene in which "theater" as well as illusion of reality is in
evidence. The actor calls attention to his acting, and the playwright invites connoisseurship of his own and the actor's techniques.

Act II develops the complication in three grandly theatrical
scenes. It begins with the trial scene in which Angelo and Escalus hear Elbow, the constable, accuse Froth of doing something
to his wife—we never learn what. Elbow is simply Dogberry
under another name, and Pompey, the bawd, obligingly drops
into the role of Verges and gives a hilarious account of Mistress
Elbow's visit to Mistress Overdone's bordello, pregnant and
"longing" for stewed prunes. This is as fine a bit of vulgar garrulity as the Nurse's account of the weaning of Juliet, or Mistress Quickly's of the death of Falstaff. Even without Professor
Kittredge's dry comments on the Elizabethan belief that prunes
were a prophylactic against the pox, it is impossible to miss the
fun of this scene, which deliberately echoes and parallels and so
recalls the Dogberry-Verges scenes in *Much Ado About Nothing*.
Not only does Elbow talk like Dogberry, and Pompey step out
of character to play up to him, but Angelo makes an impatient
departure which recalls Leonato's.

And yet this scene furthers the plot in that it shows us Angelo's
first failure as a ruler. His impatience and lack of charity ("Hop-
ing you'll find good cause to whip them all") is contrasted with
Escalus' patience in trying to discover the truth, or, failing that,
to correct the general situation. In this scene also Angelo "tempts
fate" by boasting,

> When I that censure him [Claudio] do so offend,
> Let mine own judgment pattern out my death
> And nothing come in partial. . . .   (ll. 29–31)

Viola vs Sebastine
Duke vs Friar

This is a device of foreshadowing, of pride-before-the-fall, used also especially in *Much Ado About Nothing*. It is the comic equivalent of prophecy in tragedy. The Duke had already tempted his fate and foreshadowed his proposal to Isabella by assuring Friar Thomas,

> Beleeue not that the dribling dart of Loue
> Can pierce a compleat bosome: (I, iii, 2–3. Folio, I, iv quoted).

This echo of Sidney's second sonnet would not be missed by King James, himself a sonneteer—nor by others in that first audience.[1]

The theatricality of scene ii in Act II is achieved by a different device. Isabella pleads with Angelo for her brother's life, but she is coached from the sidelines by Lucio, so that her pleading becomes a theatrical performance, something like a rehearsal, in which Lucio is the director, and the Provost, who has already made a timid effort to get a stay of execution, serves as a sympathetic audience. Isabella begins by expressing her paradoxical dilemma: a virgin, about to take a vow of perpetual chastity, forced to plead for mercy for her brother whose crime is fornication. Angelo replies curtly, "Well: the matter?" From this timid beginning, urged on by Lucio, she warms up to her argument, thinking of better and better things to say. Her first argument, "let it be his fault,/ And not my brother" who is punished, is quickly answered. But Lucio will not permit an easy surrender. "Give't not o'er so: to him again . . ." And so she goes on, "But can you if you would?" "If he had been as you, and you as he," "I would to heaven I had your potency," how would it be with you if God should "judge you as you are?" "He's not prepared for death," "Who is it that hath died for this offense?"—a question which brings Lucio's approving, "Ay, well said." So she goes on from argument to argument until she backs Angelo into a corner: "Why do you put these sayings upon me?" Her next two arguments, "Ask your heart what it doth know / That's like my brother's fault," and "Hark how I'll bribe you," bring her a disastrous victory. They force Angelo to recognize the emotion she has aroused in him. Paradoxically, her purity has aroused his libido.

The eloquence of Isabella's plea has been frequently and extravagantly admired, but the tone of the scene has been missed, at least partly because the play has been so seldom acted. While Isabella warms up to the occasion, Lucio's promptings provide a cooling, critical point of view which emphasizes her eloquence but effectively damps the emotional effect of it on the audience. Lucio is the setter-on, the coach and critic; and Isabella's plea becomes a performance. He is like a trainer in a cockfight, or a fencing match, urging her on, "give't not o'er so: to him again." "Kneel down before him, hang upon his gown." "You are too cold." "Ay, touch him; there's the vein." Finally, when Angelo says, "Well, come to me tomorrow," Lucio seizes the opportunity for a respite, snatching his cock out of the pit while the situation is still favorable, with a "Go to, 'tis well; away." The emotional response of the audience to Isabella's pleas has been conditioned and controlled by Lucio's coaching. The aim is not realism, but theater; not pathos, but paradox in making Lucio, the libertine, the coach of Isabella, the virgin, in a plea for mercy for a fornicator, a plea which arouses the judge's lust! Isabella has succeeded in setting Angelo's imagination to work; but, ironically, not in the direction she intended.

Scene iii is short, but it serves several important purposes. It shows the Duke-Friar in the prison catechizing, or "confessing" Julietta. This action has no consequence in itself, but it reminds the audience that the Duke is still in Vienna (and can reclaim his power at any moment); it shows him concerned with the spiritual needs of his subjects;[2] and it prepares us for his "consolation" of Claudio at the opening of Act III, which would otherwise, by its extreme irony and paradox, confuse the audience as to the "real" character of the Duke. The scene tells us nothing that we need to know about Julietta, but if the audience had any real fears for her lover, Claudio, the Duke's concern, and his presence on the scene and sound morality, are reassuring. Moreover, this scene makes a very necessary interval between the end of scene ii and the opening of scene iv. At the end of scene ii, after the exit of Lucio and Isabella, Angelo reveals, in soliloquy, the struggle going on in his mind. Isabella has used the conventional phrase of parting, " 'Save your honour,' " and Angelo comments when she has gone,

> From thee: even from thy virtue.
> What's this? what's this? is this her fault or mine?
> The tempter, or the tempted, who sins most?

There follows a twenty-five-line soliloquy with which scene ii ends. Scene iv opens with another soliloquy by Angelo on the same theme. Evidently Shakespeare intended to suggest that he had been wrestling with his conscience for a day, because in scene ii he bade Isabella return "tomorrow," and this second soliloquy is broken into by the announcement that she has returned. Scene iii has made the necessary diversion of interest which, in a Shakespearean play, creates the illusion of the passage of time.

Scene iv, Angelo's great scene, develops another vein of humor. Angelo is embarrassed and at a loss to know how to make his immoral proposal. At first he puts it hypothetically, asking Isabella to suppose that the only way to save Claudio's life is either to

> lay down the treasures of your body
> To this supposed, or else to let him suffer,
> What would you do?   (ll. 96–98)

Isabella replies immediately that she would die before she would "yield my body up to shame." There is a little flare of tempers as Angelo replies, "Then must your brother die," but two speeches later he scores a point and recovers his good humor. He begins again, "We are all frail," and she unwarily agrees. Immediately he suggests that she become a woman "by putting on the destined livery." Isabella does not understand him:

> I have no tongue but one. Gentle my lord,
> Let me entreat you speak the former language.

And so, finally and bluntly, he makes himself clear: "Plainly conceive, I love you." At first she sees this as a basis for further argument:

> My brother did love Juliet,
> And you tell me that he shall die for't.   (ll. 142–43)

But when she has grasped his proposal, she tries to use it to threaten him:

> I'll tell the world aloud
> What man thou art.

Angelo strikes back with confidence and some condescension (in the use of *thee*):

> Who will believe thee, Isabel?
> My unsoiled name, th'austereness of my life,
> My vouch against you, and my place i'th'state . . .

Then he threatens not only death, but torture for her brother if she refuses, ending with the demand:

> Answer me tomorrow,
> Or, by the affection that now guides me most,
> I'll prove a tyrant to him. As for you,
> Say what you can, my false o'erweighs your true.   *Exit.*

So the scene ends in mutual defiance. There is not a word of any passion except anger in it. It is a verbal duel which neither wins; for while Angelo's ultimatum is brutal, Isabella's innocence is perdurable. She is left to consider what to do next, but she never for a moment contemplates self-sacrifice. She will go to her brother with the bad news, expecting *him* to comfort *her.* She is sure he will agree that "More than our brother is our chastity." The significance of this use of the royal "our" has been pointed out.[3]

However, hers is the voice of inexperience rather than of selfishness. To her, death is no more than a word she has heard; it is not a condition she has imagined. The girlish rectitude of her reaction, its lack of compassion, or even of realization of her brother's terror, gives the audience a sense of superior wisdom which is the purest kind of pleasure. We smile at her inexperience, patronizingly, as we smile at a child's, liking her the more for it. To produce this audience-response is the very essence of comedy. So far is Isabella from the self-forgetfulness of true mercy that she is not even aware of it, and so she is charming, rather than despicable, in her innocence.[4] She has much to learn of life and suffering, and in the play she learns it quickly.

Act III consists of a single scene in two sharply contrasted parts.[5] The first part gives us Claudio's great scene. It opens in a low key with the Friar's paradoxical preparation of Claudio

for death by cataloguing the evils of life. It is put together out of
old monkish *contemptu mundi* commonplaces which, coming
from the Duke-impersonating-a-friar, are more comic than serious.
It has in it neither "the slings and arrows of outrageous fortune,"
nor any word of Christian consolation. Claudio gives appro-
priately paradoxical thanks. The Friar-Duke has ended, "Yet in
this life/Lie hid moe thousand deaths." Claudio replies:

> I humbly thank you.
> To sue to live, I find I seek to die,
> And seeking death, find life: let it come on.

At this point Isabella arrives to

> tell him of Angelo's request,
> And fit his mind to death, for his soul's rest.
>
> (II, iv, 186–87)

However, she finds this program more difficult to carry out than
she had anticipated. She begins somewhat flippantly:

> Lord Angelo, having affairs to heaven,
> Intends you for his swift ambassador . . .

But, pressed by Claudio, she admits that there is a remedy,
which she is reluctant to put into words until Claudio has assured her that he "will encounter darkness as a bride." This, and
his denunciation of Angelo, gives her courage to say:

> If I would yield him my virginity,
> Thou mightest be freed!

Claudio is properly shocked: "Thou shalt not do't," but, given
time to think, he catches at the straw of hope: "Death is a fearful
thing."

His expression of his fears has reminded many of Hamlet's

soliloquy on the same theme, and probably the reminiscence was intended, or allusive. Shakespeare repeatedly in this play echoes himself. But Claudio is no melancholy Dane. His "Ay, but to die, and go we know not where" brings him quickly to the plea: "Sweet sister, let me live." Isabella's reaction is both very human and comic. She flies into a childish rage: "O you beast, O faithless coward, O dishonest wretch!"

Although the testing of Angelo is the announced theme of the play, the testing of Isabella forms a parallel and equal counterpoise. Failure to recognize this fact has stultified both those who see her as "A thing enskied and sainted" (I, iv, 34; the words are Lucio's!), and those who think her a prude. Angelo sets out to enforce the law in Vienna with literal strictness and without the mercy which the Elizabethans, and King James, considered a part of justice. He not only fails, but he falls into the same vice which he proposes to correct, and so becomes a hypocrite and a tyrant. Isabella sets out to plead for mercy for her brother, but when she is offered it at a price, a supreme sacrifice of herself, she not only refuses to pay it but turns on her brother with rage and complete lack of mercy.

> I'll pray a thousand prayers for thy death,
> No word to save thee.   (III, i, 146–47)

This is the most passionate scene in the play, yet it has a saving element of theatricality to keep it cool (that is, in the comic mood). As Isabella enters, the Duke-Friar requests the Provost, "Bring me to hear them speak, where I may be concealed." And so the true representative of justice is present, hidden from the other actors, but not from the audience, throughout the scene. Shakespeare's audience would naturally expect the Duke (obviously no villain) to somehow save Claudio; and therefore Claudio's agonized pleading for his life would not have the same moving effect that it would have if he were really in mortal danger. Shakespeare's masterful control and modulation of audience-response is here again exhibited.

When the Friar (whom the audience knows to be the Duke) steps out of his hiding place to accost Isabella, the scene drops abruptly into prose, not because the play breaks in two at this point, as Tillyard suggested,[6] but because reason has taken over. Claudio will be saved: the only question is, how?

There is tolerance, condescension, and some irony in the words with which he accosts the angry girl, "Vouchsafe a word, young sister, but one word." . . . "The satisfaction I would require is likewise to your own benefit." Isabella is angry at Claudio, but she would like to see justice (that is, vengeance) done to Angelo; and so she readily agrees to the Friar's plan to trick him into consummating his marriage with Mariana, and at the same time, by the same trick, to secure the release of Claudio. The morality and decorum of this use of the "bed-trick" has been much discussed, but without full recognition of Mariana's dilemma. She is firmly committed to Angelo and cannot marry elsewhere while he lives, yet he "whose blood is very snow-broth" refuses to complete the marriage, and she is left marooned in her lonely grange, helpless and hopeless until the Friar brings Isabella to rescue her.[7] By arranging the substitution, Isabella will "most uprighteously do a poor wronged lady a merited benefit, redeem your brother from the angry law, do no stain to your own gracious person, and much please the absent Duke," as the Friar tells her (III, i, 196–99). He later assures Mariana:

> gentle daughter, fear you not at all;
> He is your husband on a pre-contract;

To bring you thus together, 'tis no sin,
Sith that the justice of your title to him
Doth flourish the deceit.   (IV, i, 70–74)

Isabella cannot be blamed for following the advice of one she
supposes to be a moral leader. Shakespeare has been charged
with forgetting Mariana's dignity,[8] but he saves it by indicating
that she is still in love with Angelo. In spite of his "unjust
unkindness" she "hath yet in her the continuance of her first
affection"—as the yearning of the tender little song with which
she is introduced indicates. She is twin sister of Julietta, but
Angelo's behavior is the antithesis of Claudio's. These are the
two extremes. The betrothal of the Duke and Isabella represents
the proper mean.

Throughout Act III the Duke is on stage. First there is the
dialogue between the Friar and Claudio, then that between Claudio and Isabella which the Friar overhears, then one between
the Friar and Isabella in which the substitution is arranged, and
finally what the Cambridge text designates "Scene ii" which
marks the point of no return for the minor characters. Pompey
has been arrested as a bawd. He admits the charge, but appeals
to Lucio to help him. Lucio refuses, saying instead things which
make it worse for Pompey, until we are a little sorry for him as
he is led disconsolate away to prison. Then Lucio puts himself
in trouble by telling the Friar scandal about the Duke, and immediately Mistress Overdone tells the Friar of Lucio's fathering
of Kate Keepdown's child, and so puts into his hand a whip to
punish Lucio. So the little chain of downfalls is neatly and
expeditiously arranged. In a final humorous passage the Friar
questions Escalus about the Duke's reputation and is reassured.
His crestfallen state after Lucio's scandalous report of him recalls
Benedick's similar state after Beatrice, in the masking scene,

pretends not to recognize him in his mask, and gives him a similarly unfavorable report of *his* reputation. The scene ends with a soliloquy in which the Friar throws off his pretense (perhaps removes his hood) and, as the Duke, speaks of the duty of a ruler to set a good example, and outlines his plan for correcting Angelo.

The theatricality of the last act, the play-within-a-play, stage-managed by the Duke who also plays the lead, has been recognized; but the preparation for it in Act IV has been given scant attention. In contrast to the single long scenes of Acts III and V, Act IV consists of six short scenes of rapid action. The first three move the plot along to the point where the Duke's return is necessary, and the last three show him busy preparing for it. Scene i introduces us to Mariana and provides the arrangements for the substitution of Mariana for Isabella. Isabella instructs Mariana in an off-stage interval so brief that it is filled by a six-line soliloquy in which the Friar (as Duke) meditates "O place and greatness" (ll. 59–64).[9] Short as it is, this speech serves more than one purpose. It carries the audience completely away from the business in hand, and so serves as a time interval. It reminds the audience again that the Friar is really the Duke, and it helps further to characterize the Duke.

In this scene the trap is set for Angelo. In scene ii, Pompey is persuaded to change his calling from pimp to headsman's assistant, acting out the pun on *headsman* and *maidenhead* in a bit of very masculine humor. The Provost sends Pompey to call up Claudio and Barnardine to be executed (that is, serve as pimp to the headsman).

Scene ii is the Provost's big scene, but its humor lies in the position of the Duke, whose cleverness fails, leaving him powerless because of his disguise. His own device of pretending to be a Friar, so that he can watch Angelo, renders him helpless in his opposition to Angelo's ruthless injustice. He arrives at the prison full of expectation of a pardon for Claudio. He confidently predicts to the Provost that it will come. Then the messenger arrives with the order for Claudio's execution by four (instead of the previously specified eight o'clock). Angelo orders, "Let me have Claudio's head sent me by five."

This scene is full of excitement and suspense. Twice there is a knocking at the door, and the audience is kept in a state of expectation by conversation between the Provost and the Friar, which delays the entry (ll. 63–67, 80–95). The second order for Claudio's execution not only defeats the Duke's plan but increases the urgency; but he is quick to devise a second stratagem. Barnardine is also to be executed, and on the same day. So he undertakes to persuade the Provost to send Barnardine's head instead of Claudio's. The Provost objects that this might cost him *his* head; moreover, it is against his oath of office. The Friar is forced to produce a letter in "the hand and seal of the Duke" "where you shall find within these two days he will be here." And so he hurries the Provost away because "it is almost clear dawn."

Scene iii gives the final twist to the substitution of heads. Barnardine refuses to be executed, and the Provost suggests using the head of Ragozine, who is already dead. He is off stage for nine lines while the Friar-Duke outlines quickly his plan for the Duke's return: a public entry, summoning Angelo to meet him outside the city, there

> By cold gradation and well-balanced form,
> We shall proceed with Angelo.   (ll. 90–98)

Then the Provost returns with the head and is sent to take it to Angelo. This juggling with a head is macabre humor, but it is doubly humorous because we know that it is part of a deception, a trick played on Angelo. Moreover, we have been told that the man was already dead when he was decapitated, and that he was a very wicked man, anyway. As practical stage business, this head, whether exposed or in a bag, was a familiar piece of stage property which might produce a shudder if suitably introduced, but which was certainly good for a laugh in this play. The brevity of the interval (9 lines) between the Provost's exit to get it, and his return with it ("Here is the head; I'll carry it myself") is part of the comic effect.

Two further bits of business must be run through in this scene. Isabella arrives, confident of her brother's pardon, and the Duke tells her that he has been executed, promises her revenge, and sends her to Friar Peter with a message preparing for the accusation of Angelo. Then Lucio arrives and, in indignation at Isabella's tears, and the Duke's absence which, as he thinks, has resulted in Claudio's execution, he makes further accusations against the Duke and admits that he, himself, is guilty of Claudio's offense. So his guilt is self-confessed and his punishment assured.

The last three scenes are necessary, but very short. In iv we see Escalus and Angelo, good conscience and bad, reacting to news of the Duke's return. In v, the Duke is busy sending instructions to his friends, and arranging the dramatics of his "return." He is no longer disguised in this scene, where he instructs his confidant, Friar Peter, giving him letters which he is to "at fit time deliver me," and telling him,

> The Provost knows our purpose and our plot;
> The matter being afoot, keep your instruction,
> And hold you ever to our special drift,
> Though sometimes you do blench from this to that,
> As cause doth minister.

In other words, the Duke's little drama is to be imagined as played in the style of the *commedia dell'arte*, although, of course, it is not actually so played.

The purpose of the scene is not to give the audience clues to what is coming, but merely to create expectation, to show the Duke busy at some plot or other, which arouses our curiosity and assures us that the play acting which is to follow is fully planned. Since Isabella and Mariana have parts to play, that is, must say what is not true, scene vi shows them discussing their parts after they have been coached by Friar Peter (cf. IV, iii, 135–46). "I would say the truth; but to accuse him so, / That is your part," says Isabella. The three scenes together take only sixty lines, yet they are sufficient to prepare us for Act V in which the Duke and the two women, with the aid of the Provost and Friar Peter, put on a play to reveal Angelo's duplicity and bring him to repentance and the fear of death. In Act V, only Angelo, Escalus, and Lucio are "themselves," that is, not in the Duke's confidence. The others are acting parts assigned to them.

Act V is the Duke's great scene. He enters pretending to know nothing of what has happened in his "absence," pretending full confidence in Angelo, pretending to suspect the two women who are merely following his instructions. The audience is fully aware that he is "putting on an act," but their expectation is kept up by the excitement of "why is he saying this," and "what will he do next." They are, for once, little wiser than the people on the stage. At one point the Duke resumes his role as a Friar so that Lucio can pull off his hood and reveal to the astonished actors that the Friar is really the Duke (the audience has known it all along). This little playlet is a wonderfully clever combination of two or three levels of dramaturgy, a live puppetry in which the all-knowing Duke manages the women in such a way as to force a confession from the unknowing Angelo, first in regard to Mariana (ll. 214–22) and then more fully (ll. 362–70). Even after his disguise has been pulled off, the Duke perseveres in his pretense that Claudio is dead, so that he can put the fear of death into Angelo and test Isabella's charity before restoring her brother to her.

Shakespeare is fond of having his characters put on an act, or pretend to be what the audience knows that they are not. We think immediately of Falstaff's impersonation of Hal's father, of Hero and her maids talking for Beatrice's benefit, Claudio and the Prince for Benedick's, or of Rosalind disguised as Ganymede playing that she is Rosalind to provide Orlando with practice in wooing her. *Measure for Measure,* even aside from the last act, is rich in this kind of fun. The Duke not only disguises himself as a friar but acts the part of a friar for three acts; Lucio's coaching makes an "act" of Isabella's plea for mercy for her brother; Mariana impersonates Isabella, although not on the stage. Even Pompey pretends stupid garrulity to evade Escalus' questions. The last act is merely the most elaborate and sustained bit of play acting in this very theatrical play.

It is the essence of comedy that the actors on the stage should make all kinds of mistakes and deceptions of other actors, while the audience always knows the truth. The enjoyment of great comedy lies, not in laughter, as is sometimes assumed, but in the sense of superior knowledge and intelligence which the viewer gets from observing the blunders and misunderstandings of others. He knows about Puck and the love-juice, and so the antics of the lovers and of Titania amuse him. And to be amused is not necessarily to laugh, it is to have a much deeper and more pervasive sense of well-being, of superiority, and wisdom. We observe human weakness and folly, but, like Puck, we are not of it.

We see "what fools these mortals be," and the best comedy makes us feel like superior beings. Nothing could be farther from the truth than the cliché that we "identify [ourselves] with" the characters on the stage.[10] It is our detachment which makes both the blunders of comedy and the mistakes of tragedy enjoyable, and our sense of order and "right" must be satisfied by the ending. We like to see everything straightened out or, in tragedy, to feel that we have foreseen what the end must be, being wiser than the actors in either case.

In the last act of *Measure for Measure* Shakespeare manages a *tour de force;* for the Duke's little drama involves more than the usual stage deceptions (the audience knows, but Isabella does not, that Claudio is not dead; it knows that Mariana has put Angelo into Claudio's shoes, although *he* thinks that he has done a much worse thing, deflowered Isabella and executed Claudio). Shakespeare has gone much farther than this. He not only has some of the actors playing parts for the benefit of others, the purposes and outcome of which the actors themselves do not know, but also he keeps the audience in ignorance and therefore in suspense to the very last moment. We know, in general, what the Duke's aim is—to bring Angelo to justice. It is necessary, therefore, that the audience have complete confidence in the ability and virtue of the Duke, and this confidence has been firmly built, from the first scene, at least for King James and his court, partly by echoes of the King's own declaration of his principles,[11] but partly, even for a modern audience, by the Duke's concern for good government, his presence in Vienna, and his adroitness in saving Isabella's chastity and Claudio's life, a proof of ability which assures us that he will succeed in whatever he is doing in Act V, although just what he is doing, and why he is doing it, is not apparent until his strategy has succeeded and the play is at an end.

This preservation of suspense until the very last moment is one of the marvels of the play. We have only to compare Act V with the last act of the *Comedy of Errors* to see how good it is. All the elements of the Duke's little play point to the judgment of Angelo, and the deliberate ambiguity of the title, *Measure for Measure*,[12] helps (like a false clue in a mystery story) to keep the outcome from being prematurely obvious. The ending is, therefore, more delightful in its rightness than we had been led to expect. The Duke puts Angelo in Claudio's shoes, not only making him repent (he has done that already), but teaching him forbearance as well, by putting him in exactly the same position as the man he has condemned and thinks he has executed. It is a trick very similar to the one used by the Duke of Milan to bring his brother to repentance at the climax of *The Tempest*. For Isabella, the Duke's little play is more properly a test, but she has been adequately prepared for passing it, as we shall see presently.

IV · Paradox, Macabre Humor, and Suspense

Comedy is not made by plot alone, but by the total product of the poet's conception—plot, character, dialogue, scene arrangement: all the devices of rhetoric as of theater. *Measure for Measure* is a highly sophisticated and witty play, not only deliberately and obviously theatrical, but full of irony, paradox, and contrived suspense.

The plot is based on the paradox of a law that punishes the man rather than the woman for adultery. Old Testament law and universal custom punished the woman severely. The "law of Vienna" condemned the man to death but spared the woman with a lesser penalty. Shakespeare goes further and shows Julietta being cared for, both physically and spiritually. He has turned the traditional mores upside down, basing the play on a reversal of what is usual and expected. This paradox was inherent in the old plot, but he emphasized it and supplemented it with other paradoxes. Isabella the chaste is embarrassed at having to plead for mercy for her brother who has been unchaste (II, ii,

29–33). It is her purity which tempts Angelo to lust. He laments
the paradox, saying:

> Can it be
> That modesty may more betray our sense
> Than woman's lightness? . . .
> Dost thou desire her foully for those things
> That make her good? . . .
> O cunning enemy that, to catch a saint,
> With saints dost bait thy hook: most dangerous
> Is that temptation that doth goad us on
> To sin in loving virtue.   (II, ii, 168–83)

Angelo, "a man whose blood/ Is very snow-broth" (I, iv, 57–58),
is suddenly overwhelmed with desire for Isabella.

In addition to these and other major paradoxes in the plot,
there is much paradoxical phrasing in the play's witty dialogue.
Lucio says, more truly than he knows, that in abdicating the
Duke has "usurped the beggary he was never born to" (III, ii,
88). "Some rise by sin, and some by virtue fall," observed Escalus
(II, i, 38). The Duke admonishes Angelo not "to waste/ Thyself
upon thy virtues, they on thee" (I, i, 30–31). Later the Duke
assures Escalus, "there is so great a fever on goodness that the
dissolution of it must cure it." He adds, "Novelty is only in
request, and it is as dangerous to be aged in any kind of course
as it is virtuous to be constant in any undertaking" (that is, it is
dangerous to be constant although constancy is a virtue; III, ii,
209–17). The Duke observes:

> When vice makes mercy, mercy's so extended
> That for the fault's love is th' offender friended.
>   (IV, ii, 108, 109)

Indeed, the paradoxes of speech and situation are pervasive from
the opening scene to the last, where Lucio, the most hoodwinked

of them all, is the one who pulls the hood from the head of the Duke, the one person who is unhoodwinked (that is, has full knowledge). Isabella the chaste arranges Mariana's assignation with her affianced husband. Pompey the bawd turns headsman's assistant, or bawd to the headsman, and is sent to call Claudio, a fornicator, to be beheaded. The Friar, a "holy" man, gives pagan consolation to Claudio phrased paradoxically as contempt for life, and Claudio renders paradoxical thanks:

> To sue to live, I find I seek to die,
> And, seeking death, find life: let it come on.
>
> (III, i, 42–43)

The play is almost as rich in paradoxes as Donne's "Divine Poems."

We must regard as sheer genius the leap of the imagination which associated the old tale of a sister's sacrifice to save her brother with the meaning of Christmas; but having made the electric arc, Shakespeare has exploited his materials with more than his usual deftness. He has used his plot not only to develop paradox and irony, but to give his work masculine vigor and intensity by developing the inherent suspense and grim humor of the situation, as well. To put it another way, Shakespeare has used a plot which involves the greatest of all fears, the fear of death. It is this extreme seriousness of the situation which has done much to persuade modern critics that the play is "realistic" —that and less confidence in justice human and divine than the Elizabethans seem to have felt. But serious situations have been exploited for comic ends elsewhere, as, for example, in *The Beggar's Opera*. The presence on the scene of the Duke, whose mercifulness is clear from the beginning, was sufficient assurance of a solution of all difficulties for that first audience. It might be so for us if we could recognize in the Duke a delegated authority which made him "like power divine."

It is probable, too, that the kind of humor which pervades the play, and which has so disquieted modern critics, was more common then than now. Professor Kittredge used to say jocosely that Shakespearean jokes could be divided into two classes, scatologic and pornographic (the pox and horns); but there is a third kind exploited in both his comedies and his tragedies. Macabre humor involves a shock of horror which incites its own kind of laughter. We think immediately of poor Yorick's skull and the discussion of Hamlet's question, "How long will a man lie i'the earth ere he rot?" Macabre jokes are pervasive in *Measure for Measure,* not only in the juggling with heads, but in the flippancy of the remarks about Claudio's predicament, from Mistress Overdone's announcement, "I saw him arrested, saw him carried away, and, which is more, within these three days his head to be chopped off" (I, ii, 63–65), to Lucio's "thy head stands so tickle on thy shoulders that a milkmaid, if she be in love, may sigh it off" (I, ii, 167–69) and "I would be sorry [your head] should be thus foolishly lost at a game of tick-tack" (I, ii, 184–85).

This type of humor occurs also in the romantic comedies. One of the most outrageous examples serves as the turning point in *A Winter's Tale.* It is not by accident, ignorance, or indifference that Shakespeare gives Bohemia a seacoast. He wants the Bohemia where Antigonus is pursued and eaten by a bear to be removed from reality even farther than the woods of Bottom's transfiguration. The death of Antigonus is an excursion into an especially hilarious field of comedy—hilarious because the grim reality of death has cut through the artifice of the plot and left us surprised to laughter by sheer absurdity or incongruity. "Thou

art perfect then, our ship hath touch'd upon/ The deserts of
Bohemia?" This is a perfect opening for what follows, Antigonus'
absurd account of the visit of Hermione's ghost, as prelude and
preparation for his own absurd demise:

> To me comes a creature,
> Sometimes her head on one side, some another;
> I never saw a vessel of like sorrow,
> So fill'd and so becoming. In pure white robes,
> Like very sanctity, she did approach
> My cabin where I lay; thrice bow'd before me,
> And, gasping to begin some speech, her eyes
> Became two spouts; . . .

Then she speaks:

> Good Antigonus,
> Since fate, against thy better disposition,
> Hath made thy person for the thrower-out
> Of my poor babe, . . .   (III, iii, 19–30)[1]

Note the utter conventionality of the apparition's appearance
and behavior, and the progressive absurdity of the choice of
epithets, "creature," "vessel," "spouts," "the thrower-out"! This is
the use of incongruity to block sympathy and provoke laughter.
Antigonus is a dullard who believes that the child is "indeed the
issue of King Polixenes," and for this false judgment he is
promptly and extravagantly punished; but quite impersonally
(like Little Red Riding Hood's grandmother), *"Exit, pursued by
a bear."* It has the unreality of the kind of fiction where our
sense of reality is consciously suspended and so ambivalent, or
rather ambicredulous (if I may coin a word). We laugh even
while we shudder at the clown's report of seeing "the bear half
din'd on the gentleman. He's at it now." (III, iii, 108–9)

In the first comic scene of *Measure for Measure* (I, ii) Shake-speare begins with jokes that are largely echoes of his earlier plays, especially of the tavern scenes of the *Henry IV* plays. We recognize the puns on "grace," on "piled velvet," and on the effects of the pox: baldness (a French crown), hollow bones, etc. The pleasure invited is of recognition (not, as with original puns, of surprise) and of expectation of fun such as those earlier plays provided. These stale jokes also serve to characterize the idle crew being introduced. They set the tone of the scene in which Claudio appears for the first time and states his case. His grave trouble, and serious statement of it, contrasts with their flippancy, as his blank-verse lines contrast with their prose, but his indignation at the sudden revival of "the drowsy and neglected act" averts over-sympathy. The effect is of irony, not of tragedy.

Other strains of humor are exploited in other scenes, but that in IV, iii is as genuinely and effectively macabre as anything in Shakespeare:

Pompey. Master Barnardine, you must rise and be hanged, Master Barnardine.

.   .   .

Pray, Master Barnardine, awake till you are executed, and sleep afterwards.

Then, as Barnardine enters, Abhorson asks Pompey, "Is the axe upon the block, sirrah?"

Pompey. Very ready, sir.
Barnardine. How now, Abhorson, what's the news with you?
Abhorson. Truly, sir, I would desire you to clap into your prayers: for look you, the warrant's come.
Barnardine. You rogue, I have been drinking all night; I am not fitted for't.

he better, sir: for he that drinks all night, and is hanged
e morning, may sleep the sounder all the next day.

(ll. 20–44)

Barnardine's resolute refusal to be executed is at once grim and
absurd. Pompey's joke makes it impossible to give the situation
our sympathy. We are reminded that this is a *play* even while
it simulates reality.

There is, of course, a connection between macabre humor and
suspense. Because of the threatened finality of death, the vivid-
ness of the play, that is, the suspense of the audience, is kept
taut throughout. The jokes about death help to keep it imminent
while dissipating the awe and fear which normally accompany it.
The matter-of-fact treatment of it contributes both to the humor
and to the suspense.

One of the most brilliant technical achievements of *Measure
for Measure* is the sustaining of tension. In tragedy, suspense is
created by the expectation of dire events, an expectation based on
a causal chain, which should seem to lead inevitably to the
catastrophe. In comedy, surprise plays a more considerable part
in arousing and sustaining interest. We are kept attentive by the
accidental and unpredictable, as well as by mistakes and confu-
sions arising from the characters' ignorance or misapprehension.
It is well known that Shakespeare was especially fond of mistaken identity as a source of comic situation, as here in Lucio's
mistake in abusing the Duke to the Friar and the Friar to the
Duke. But any kind of ignorance on the part of a character on
the stage, ignorance which the audience does not share, is useful:
Angelo's ignorance of the presence of the Duke in Vienna; Isabella's ignorance of men, in her dealing with both Angelo and
Claudio; Claudio's and Isabella's ignorance of the identity of the

Friar; and so on. Even while we are enjoying our superior knowledge or judgment, we feel a thrill of anticipation of the consequences of this mistake or ignorance.

Sometimes Shakespeare builds suspense to an almost intolerable
height, as in *King Lear* when Edmund and Edgar fight and then
talk while the audience waits, knowing that Lear and Cordelia
have been captured and that the order for their immediate execution has been given. The tension is so great that we are tempted
to shout at Edgar and Kent, "Look to Lear and Cordelia!" When
Lear finally reappears with Cordelia in his arms our first reaction
is one of relief. Lear is still alive (we do not yet know that
Cordelia is dead). This is the suspense of waiting for an expected
event. Usually it is greater in tragedy than in comedy because
the consequences expected are more grave, but in *Measure for
Measure* Claudio's sentence of death hangs over the first four
acts, and expectation of Angelo's punishment over the fifth act,
and while we do not actually expect the finality of death in
either case, we get almost the same thrill from the threat of it;
as we thrill at the plunge and soar of a roller coaster in an amusement park which gives us the excitement without the reality of
danger. So in this play Shakespeare uses the threat of death to
create suspense of almost tragic intensity, even while the ubiquity
of the merciful Duke makes tragic catastrophe improbable.

Shakespeare had a special problem in creating and maintaining
suspense in this play, because in altering the old plot from tragicomedy to pure comedy he destroyed the old sources of suspense.
The heroine no longer had an internal conflict and made no
sacrifice such as made death welcome to Whetstone's Cassandra,
and there were elements of surprise in the judgments of the
Emperor which gave Whetstone's plot at least a what-will-happen-
next kind of suspense. All this Shakespeare abandoned when he

began with the good ruler and made Isabella's predicament comic, instead of tragic. The Duke's presence in Vienna and his benevolent character assured a happy ending from the start, but any plot must have suspense, and so Shakespeare makes use of the pressure of time and the surprises of witty talk and theatrical effect to replace the old melodramatic tensions.

Everything is to happen "tomorrow." He had used the pressure of time rather ineffectively in the *Comedy of Errors,* where, in the first scene, Aegeon is sentenced to die at sundown if help does not come. However, in the complications of mistaken identity which follow, we forget Aegeon until he reappears in the denouement. In *Measure for Measure* the pressure of time is used much more skillfully. The need for haste is suggested even as the plot is being set in motion in the first act. Claudio tells Lucio, "This day my sister should the cloister enter" (I, ii, 172), and Lucio tells Isabella that Angelo

> has censured him [Claudio]
> Already and, as I hear, the provost hath
> A warrant for his execution.   (I, iv, 72–74)

Beginning in the first scene of Act II, the pressure of time increases. Claudio is to be executed "by nine tomorrow morning" (II, i, 34). We are startled when, in the next scene, in reply to Isabella's pleas, Angelo tells her, "Come to me tomorrow . . . At any time 'fore noon" (ii, 155, 160). Those in the audience who recognized the old story (and we can surely assume that many did), would remember the Deputy's treachery and anticipate it here, and so be pleasantly surprised when Isabella returns in II, iv. We naturally suppose that it is the next day (day 2), yet Claudio is still alive. In this scene Isabella is defeated in her argument with Angelo and he orders her, "Answer me tomorrow"

(II, iv, 167). The next scene shows us Claudio being prepared for death by the Friar, and Isabella tells him, "Tomorrow you set on" (III, i, 61). The Friar too says, "Tomorrow you must die" (l. 168). When Isabella talks with Mariana we must assume that it is day 3, since she has already seen Angelo a third time to make arrangements for the assignation. It must be the early morning of day 4, therefore, when the treacherous order for the execution of Claudio "by four of the clock" is brought to the prison (IV, ii, 117). In the next scene, after the substitute head has been sent to Angelo, the Friar tells Isabella, "The Duke comes home tomorrow" (IV, iii, 125). And so, by a neat juggling of "tomorrows," Shakespeare creates the sense of urgency which he needs for suspense.

Moreover, this tension of urgency is increased in Act III when the Friar takes command of the situation. Having failed to persuade Angelo to pardon her brother, Isabella next fails to persuade her brother to die to preserve her chastity. The Friar, therefore, has the double problem of relieving these two failures. The dexterity with which he produces Mariana would be deplorable in a tragedy, since there has been no preparation for it, no causal link, except the emphasis on Angelo's general coldness of temperament. In comedy it is simply a delightful surprise, a clever ruse, by which Isabella's virginity is preserved. Events move very rapidly thereafter. In IV, i Mariana is instructed, and in IV, ii the Friar appears in the jail confidently predicting Claudio's pardon (ll. 104 ff.). Instead of this pardon, the order for execution is repeated, naming an earlier hour, and the Friar is put to desperate shifts to save him. These shifts, the need to persuade the honest Provost to cooperate, increase the urgency which Shakespeare emphasizes by several references to the pressure of time.

However, the moment the Duke resumes authority, as he does at the opening of Act V, this tension is entirely relieved. There is need only for explanations all around of what the audience already knows (and punishment of Angelo), and this is pretty dull, as the last act of the *Comedy of Errors* shows. But in *Measure for Measure* Shakespeare has translated his exposition into further action. He has made a long denouement dramatic and filled with suspense, by the device of having the Duke arrange and produce a play which brings Angelo to full repentance and teaches both Angelo and Isabella that human justice includes mercy. To this end it is necessary that both should believe Claudio to be dead. First Angelo's guilt as a seducer is revealed, and he is let off with marriage to Mariana. Then he is accused of the murder of Claudio, so that Isabella can be brought to plead for his life. Then, at last, Claudio is reunited with his sister and his Julietta.

The judgments which finally determine the fate of all the important characters are spoken in the last twenty lines of the play, beginning with Lucio's sentence "to marry a punk," then Claudio's to marry Julietta and Angelo's to love Mariana. Escalus is promised reward for his goodness, Angelo is ordered to forgive the Provost, and finally the Duke makes formal proposal of marriage to Isabella, and a concluding couplet sweeps the stage.

This is all very neat and workmanlike, but before he can pronounce these "sentences" the Duke must put on his play. Up to the point where Lucio pulls off the Friar's hood and reveals to the other characters on the stage that the Friar is really the Duke in disguise, the Duke has been pretending that he has just returned from a journey and that he knows nothing about what has happened in his absence, pretending complete confidence in Angelo.

In order to appreciate this play-acting on the part of the Duke, we must consider its dramatic effectiveness. Since the audience could have no doubt that, when he "returned," the Duke would restore justice with mercy to Vienna, the first effect of his entrance must be surprise at his warm greeting of Angelo:

> We have made inquiry of you, and we hear
> Such goodness of your justice, that our soul
> Cannot but yield you forth to public thanks,
> Forerunning more requital.   (ll. 5–8)

This is dissimulation. He is lying, as the audience knows, and the effect of his deception is to encourage Angelo to lie also to cover his wickedness. But Isabella, who now appears to plead her grievance against Angelo, also lies, as the audience knows, when she says, "And I did yield to him" (l. 101). The Duke refuses to believe her and asks who "knew of your intent and coming hither?" (l. 124), and she names the Friar. This is amusing in itself to an audience that knows the Duke was the Friar, but it is exploited further by having Lucio break in, to abuse the Friar to the Duke as he had previously abused the Duke to the Friar. This is hilariously funny and, with his usual tact in judging the duration of a dramatic moment and stopping well short of satiety, Shakespeare, after two speeches of Lucio's, has Friar Peter come to the defense of Friar Lodowick and accuse Isabella (rightly) of lying. Then Mariana is brought in and makes her charge against Angelo, telling the truth about the assignation, and so refuting Isabella's charge. Angelo thinks that *she* is lying, and so is emboldened to deny the whole thing, asking:

> Let me have way, my lord,
> To find this practice out.   (ll. 236–37)

As a piece of strategy on the part of a ruler, this is clever. Step by step he is entrapping Angelo while pretending full confidence in him, encouraging him to think that he can brazen it out, so that when the moment of truth comes Angelo will have no shadow of defense left. The Duke can turn to him with the stern words:

> Hast thou or word, or wit, or impudence
> That yet can do thee office?   (ll. 359–60)

and Angelo can only reply:

> O my dread lord,
> I should be guiltier than my guiltiness
> To think I can be undiscernible,
> When I perceive your grace, like power divine,
> Hath looked upon my passes.

Having sent Angelo off to be married to Mariana, the Duke now turns to Isabella, but he is not yet through with his stratagems. He cannot yet tell her that her brother lives, because he is not yet through with Angelo. He has to charge him with the "double violation of sacred chastity, and of promise-breach" and order his execution; so that, first, he can put Angelo in the same jeopardy in which Angelo put Claudio, and second, he can then offer Isabella a chance for vengeance, "An Angelo for Claudio, death for death!" (l. 405). This, again, is strategy, what King James called "kingcraft."

The whole act is a revelation, and demonstration, of the Duke's cleverness as a ruler as well as of Shakespeare's cleverness as a playwright. The center of interest has shifted from the predicament of Claudio and the trial of Isabella to the Duke, his ability to manipulate his subjects, and his resourcefulness in meeting situations. The shift takes place, of course, at the usual place in a

Shakespearean play, the beginning of Act IV; but in Act IV the
Duke is exceedingly busy meeting emergencies and averting
disaster. In Act V he administers justice, not by the simple and
direct exercise of power and force, but by sheer cleverness in
the management of people. It is this cleverness which holds the
audience in suspense throughout the last act. The deceptions,
the unexpected turns of events, arouse surprised interest. The
audience is tantalized by the behavior of the Duke and Isabella.
Curiosity is raised to fever heat by the unexpected, and the Duke
is so thoroughly in command that his pretenses and even his
temporary injustice, in turning Isabella and Mariana over to
Angelo for investigation, become elements in an almost intolerable suspense. Up to this point we have enjoyed the ignorance
and mistakes of the characters on stage, since our knowledge is
superior to theirs. But suddenly, in Act V, the audience is made
to share with the actors ignorance of the purport of what they
see and hear. The Duke becomes dramatist, assuming a part and,
with the cooperation of several who have been coached in advance (Isabella, Mariana, the Provost, and Friar Peter), putting
on a play which is as surprising to the audience, in spite of their
superior knowledge, as it is to the other actors on the stage. It is
this element of surprise, of admiration for cleverness, and of
superb showmanship in action, which creates the suspense of the
last act, a suspense paced and heightened by Lucio's constant
interruptions—but of that more later.

V · Isabella

In the general assault on the play almost every one of the characters has been singled out for denigration, but the one considered central, the one who is supposed to have a "real life problem" is Isabella, and so a veritable war has been waged over her. The characters of the other principals, Angelo, Claudio, and even the Duke, are dictated to a considerable extent by the necessities of the plot; but Isabella, by breaking out of the old pattern, becomes a formative influence on the action and so must be understood. Here critics and theorists have done their worst. She has been described as a saint, an angel of mercy confronted with an impossible dilemma. Professor Bullough points out that, unlike her predecessors, she is "a novice." He concludes: "Make her a novice however, austere and prevented from leaving the world only by her brother's danger, and her refusal becomes inevitable, his demand outrageous . . . the law she serves is one above Nature; and she conquers in the struggle between natural affection and supernatural injunctions. By so doing she passes into an order of imaginative conception different from that of Shakespeare's previous heroines of comedy. She transcends the part she has henceforth to play, and it is with some hesitation that the dramatist hints at the end that the Duke will formally

ask her to marry him." [1] So it might have been, but is that really
the Isabella Shakespeare has given us? On the other hand, Sir
Arthur Quiller-Couch finds her "somewhat rancid in her chastity.
. . . all for saving her own soul, and she saves it by turning, of a
sudden, into a bare procuress." [2] Both of these judgments are
predicated on the theory that this is "a play dealing seriously
[i.e., literally] with the problems of life," [3] and that Isabella's
problem is central to the play. Every serious piece of literature
must deal with "the problems of life," with human affairs, but
the literal way of realism is only one of several ways in which,
and by which, literature deals with life. If we try to interpret the
play on this literal level as a picture of "real life," if we grant
that "it presents one of those dreadful alternatives between con-
flicting demands of honor and affection which have in them the
very essence of tragic drama," [4] we should be struck by the fact
that Isabella is entirely unconscious of any such alternative. She
never, for a single line, contemplates or debates with herself any
such choice. When Angelo finally makes her understand his
offer,

> *Angelo.* Plainly conceive, I love you.
> *Isabella.* My brother did love Juliet,
>   And you tell me that he shall die for't.
> *Angelo.* He shall not, Isabel, if you give me love,

she at first disbelieves, and then threatens him:

> I will proclaim thee, Angelo, look for't!
> Sign me a present pardon for my brother,
> Or with an outstretched throat I'll tell the world . . . .
>   (II, iv, 141–53)

This is her position, and she never wavers from it. She has no
problem, because she sees no alternative. She has no struggle

except the external struggle of wills with Angelo, and then with Claudio, a struggle which is completed in Act III.

Moreover, if we try to interpret this play on the level of "real life" we must observe that the Duke set out to correct (through Angelo) the sex morality of Vienna, and that at the end of the play the only solution offered consists of several marriages and a general atmosphere of forgiveness all around. We are right back where we started as far as the Duke's government is concerned. In the repentance of Angelo and the reformation of Isabella we have a much more satisfactory ending, and this is the surprise Shakespeare has for his audience. We have been partly prepared for Angelo's repentance by the mental struggle he experiences over his lust for Isabella, and by his uneasiness over the news that the Duke is returning. He is not quite a monster, although his going through with the assignation, and then treacherously ordering the execution of Claudio puts us so out of sympathy with him that his reclamation stretches our charity to welcome it and suggests that the Divine Mercy is greater than mere humans can understand.

We have also been prepared for the reform of Isabella—but rather as a detective story prepares us for its denouement, so ambiguously, so indirectly, that we perceive it as we see clues in the detective story, only in retrospect. The playwright has other concerns than the taming of Isabella, although he does not neglect that strand in his elaborate tapestry. There is hardly even a clue to the Duke's falling in love with her, except in his defiance of Cupid in Act I, scene iii. Yet it is made credible by her girlish charm. Isabella, in spite of her prudery and her self-righteousness, has all the charm of innocent girlhood. And to Shakespeare and his audience (as to all true Protestants and many Catholics today) providing the Duke with an heir was surely a better fate than

being a nun, or, as Beatrice puts it, leading apes in Hell. Isabella
is not yet in love, of course, but in the Elizabethan world love
comes more properly after marriage than before. Her obedience
to the Friar presages a happy marriage to the Duke. Even Angelo,
now that his vulnerability to love has been revealed to him, will,
we can reasonably assume, cherish his wife, as we hope that
Bertram will respect and cherish Helena. Repentance "is nothing
but heart-sorrow and a clear life ensuing." In other words, reformation is implicit in true repentance.

Curiously enough, in all the discussions of Isabella's character,
from Mrs. Jameson's dithyrambics to Quiller-Couch's vilification
and R. W. Chambers' eloquent if excessive defense, there has
been no analysis of the opening scenes, and no mention of Lucio's
part in them. As a result of this oversight it was possible for
Tillyard to say, "There is no more independent character in
Shakespeare than the Isabella of the first half of the play. . . .
The essence of her disposition is decision," but in the middle of
Act III, when the Duke takes charge, "she proceeds to exchange
her native ferocity [sic!] for the hushed and submissive tones of
a well-trained confidential secretary." [5]

On the contrary, in her first two appearances, where her character is being established, she is neither independent and decisive,
nor "ferocious." She is yielding, submissive, feminine, and youthful. We see her first with a nun, inquiring about the "privileges"
of the "votarists of Saint Clare" (an order of nuns famous for
the strictness of its rule), and "wishing a more strict restraint"—
like a romantic schoolgirl. Lucio arrives to tell her of her brother's
predicament and to enlist her help. He ends:

> All hope is gone,
> Unless you have the grace by your fair prayer
> To soften Angelo.   (I, iv, 68–70)

Isabella responds:

> Alas, what poor ability's in me
> To do him good?
> *Lucio.*   Assay what power you have.
> *Isabella.* My power? Alas, I doubt. . . .   (ll. 75–77)

It takes Lucio's assurance that "when maidens sue,/ Men give like gods" to bring her to the decision, "I'll see what I can do." Once she has made up her mind, she acts promptly.

> I will about it straight.
> No longer staying but to give the Mother
> Notice of my affair. I humbly thank you;
> Commend me to my brother; soon at night
> I'll send him certain word of my success.   (ll. 85–89)

That is, I will let him know definitely how I succeed. We might imagine her as going alone straight to Angelo and there making her plea for mercy. But that is not the way Shakespeare represents her. When next she appears, in II, ii, 26 ff., Lucio is with her, and her opening is apologetic and timid. Angelo greets her with "Y' are welcome:/ What's your will?" She replies humbly:

> I am a woeful suitor to your honor,
> Please but your honor hear me.

Angelo is impatient. "Well: what's your suit?" She begins feebly:

> There is a vice that most I do abhor,
> And most desire should meet the blow of justice,
> For which I would not plead, but that I must,
> For which I must not plead, but that I am
> At war 'twixt will and will not.

Evidently, she has had misgivings and does not know what to say next. Angelo snaps at her, "Well: the matter?" and she tries again:

> I have a brother is condemned to die.
> I do beseech you, let it be his fault,
> And not my brother.

This bit of sophistry Angelo answers promptly, and Isabella responds weakly:

> O just but severe law!
> I had a brother then; heaven keep your honor.

She seems to be resigned until Lucio steps in to urge her to make another effort, to show more feeling.

> Give't not o'er so: to him again, entreat him,
> Kneel down before him, hang upon his gown;
> You are too cold. If you should need a pin,
> You could not with more tame a tongue desire it;
> To him, I say.

Thus commanded, Isabella tries again; but four exchanges later, Lucio repeats, "You are too cold." Although she begins to warm up as Lucio continues to encourage her, hers is not a spontaneous but a coached performance. Isabella is as much acting under the direction of Lucio in this scene as she will be under the direction of the Friar later.

That is not to say that she is a mere puppet, without initiative or will of her own. She is a young girl, inexperienced, pliable, simple and direct in her actions and reactions. In her second interview with Angelo, since no third party is, or can be, present, Angelo himself is forced by her timidity to encourage her. He greets her, "How now, fair maid!" and she replies primly, "I am come to know your pleasure." Angelo responds, "Your brother cannot live," and she says submissively, "Even so: heaven keep your honor." So Angelo hints at a reprieve. "Yet may he live a while; . . ." Isabella merely inquires when he must die:

> When, I beseech you? that in his reprieve,
> Longer or shorter, he may be so fitted
> That his soul sicken not.

Angelo's first problem, in this scene, is to combat her resignation, to put her in a frame of mind to make some effort to save her brother. Throughout the scene, however, down to line 149, when she finally understands Angelo's proposal, she is passive, offering no argument. She is firm only on one point: "I had rather give my body than my soul." Angelo cannot even make her understand what he is proposing, and he loses patience,

> Nay, but hear me;
> Your sense pursues not mine: either you are ignorant,
> Or seem so craftily; and that's not good.   (ll. 73–75)

Baffled by her failure to understand his indirections, he finally puts his proposition in the form of a hypothetical case. She replies unhesitatingly that she would do as much for her brother as for herself, she would submit to death by torture "ere I'ld yield/ My body up to shame" (l. 103). On this point she is adamant as a well-schooled girl. Angelo's plainer statement of his intentions only produces a flare of temper when she threatens to "tell on him." She is really helplessly inadequate to meet the situation, and when Angelo delivers his ultimatum and departs, her soliloquy is touching in its childishness:

> To whom should I complain? Did I tell this,
> Who would believe me?   (ll. 171–72)

She is echoing Angelo's "Who will believe thee, Isabel?" Her prototype in Cintio and Whetstone unaided makes her decision to appeal to superior authority, emperor or king, but Isabella has no resources of resolution as she has none of experience. After five lines of meditation, generalizing on her experience of Angelo, she decides with pitiful naïveté,

> I'll to my brother
> Though he hath fall'n by prompture of the blood,
> Yet hath he in him such a mind of honor
> That, had he twenty heads to tender down
> On twenty bloody blocks, he'ld yield them up,
> Before his sister should her body stoop
> To such abhorred pollution.

And so, having found (in her inexperience with life and people) another man to direct her course, she recovers her spirits.

> Then, Isabel, live chaste, and, brother, die:
> More than our brother is our chastity.
> I'll tell him yet of Angelo's request,
> And fit his mind to death, for his soul's rest.   *Exit.*

However, that is too much to expect of any brother, as she soon discovers. Claudio is human, and life has not yet humanized Isabella. She does not know the meaning of death, nor, therefore, of life; but she is charming rather than despicable in her innocence. She has much to learn of compassion, and she must learn by suffering. Her fury at her brother for letting her down begins the process of humanizing her, and the Friar's greeting reflects an adult's amused tolerance of her childishness: "Vouchsafe a word, young sister, but one word." (III, i, 152)

Isabella is neither an angel of mercy, a proto-nun, nor a prude. She is a young and inexperienced girl with all the charm of girlish innocence about her, and all the romantic notions of girlhood about honor and virginity. She is, by nature, yielding, submissive, whether to Lucio or Angelo or the Friar, except when her ideals and illusions are threatened. Like a very woman, she longs to submit herself, and so she would join a religious order. There is more of Hero or Cordelia about her than of Viola or Portia. Like Desdemona and Cordelia, she speaks little except under the compulsion of necessity. Her acquiescence and short speeches, in the second interview with Angelo up to the point where she realizes what he is proposing, should adequately prepare us for her silences and her submissiveness in the latter half of the play.

She has been charged with being a prude, a hypocrite in arranging for Mariana to do what she will not do herself, a vain woman in accepting part of the blame for Angelo's downfall— and she is blamed for not going back to her nunnery at the end. The first and last charge rather cancel each other out, but, if we allow Isabella youth and innocence, her concern for her virginity becomes very natural and normal. The resolution to enter a nunnery, while it was anachronistic in Shakespeare's England, is a simple device for objectifying and dramatizing the representation of natural reluctance in a modest maiden who has not yet fallen in love. Angelo at no point woos her or attempts to seduce her. His proposal is kept impersonal. We have only to think of Richard's wooing of Anne, in *Richard III,* to realize how thoroughly the scene is one of comic device, not of tragic "realism." In addition, for those who recognized the old plot, Shakespeare added the comic element of surprise. How startling that Isabella should refuse to save her brother! Here is an impasse: what will happen now?

Isabella's hypocrisy disappears with her prudery. Mariana's is a hopeless and helpless situation until Isabella rescues her. We must remember too that it is a friar, a "holy father" (so far as she knows), who suggests the substitution and justifies the ethics of it. If her decision to become a nun is no more than a normal dramatizing of her natural modesty and virginity, then her decision to help Mariana to a husband is also a natural and pleasing, because generous, impulse. However, there is another element in this decision which is less admirable. She has just responded to Claudio's plea, "Sweet sister, let me live!" with an outraged cry, "O you beast,/ O faithless coward, O dishonest wretch!" ending spitefully, "I'll pray a thousand prayers for thy death,/ No word to save thee." (III, i, 136–37, 146–47)

She does not love her brother as herself. The Friar-Duke's judgment of the situation is implied in the words with which he accosts her, saying, "Might you dispense with your leisure, I would by and by have some speech with you: the satisfaction I would require is likewise your own benefit" (III, i, 154–56). She has no sympathy for Claudio, at the moment, because she is thinking only of herself; but she would like to take vengeance on Angelo, and so she readily agrees to the Friar's plan to trick him into consummating his marriage to Mariana. It is this all-too-human desire to strike back at Angelo which justifies the Friar's cruel deception later, when he tells her falsely that Claudio is dead.

She has been accused, because she says nothing, of failing to greet Claudio when he is revealed in the last scene; but the action indicated is eloquent enough, and we are prepared for it by her tears when she is first told that he is dead. Lucio protests that her eyes are red (IV, iii). Grief matures her sympathies and humbles her pride so that, when the second test of her charity comes, she can understand Mariana's anguish at the prospect of losing her newly gained husband, and Angelo's predicament which is so like her brother's, and she will kneel beside Mariana and plead for the life of her enemy. She can put herself in Mariana's place (having suffered. the grief of a similar loss), and she can see Angelo in her brother's place and be generous.

Her plea is a wonderful speech, wrung from her in grief and understanding. These, her last words in the play, are her most eloquent. The broken lines and simple, abrupt phrasing suggest how hard they are to say:

> Most bounteous sir,
> Look, if it please you, on this man condemned
> As if my brother lived. I partly think
> A due sincerity governèd his deeds
> Till he did look on me. Since it is so,
> Let him not die; my brother had but justice,
> In that he did the thing for which he died.
> For Angelo,
> His act did not o'ertake his bad intent,
> And must be buried but as an intent
> That perished by the way. Thoughts are no subjects,
> Intents but merely thoughts.[6]   (V, i, 439–49)

Isabella has actually been blamed for vanity because she takes on herself a share of the blame by saying, "till he did look on me." This is merely and simply the truth. She is being scrupulously honest. She has been to the hard school of experience, and she has grown up from the girlish idealism which longed for a stricter nunnery, and the self-righteousness of "More than our brother is our chastity," to the position on her knees beside Mariana, pleading for the life of her enemy.

The Duke does not make it easy for her. He urges her to demand "An Angelo for Claudio, death for death!" This is the

"measure for measure" of the old Law of "an eye for an eye,
a tooth for a tooth." [7] But Isabella has learned, through grief,
the New Law: "Judge not, that ye be not judged. For with what
judgment ye judge, ye shall be judged: and with what measure
ye meet, it shall be measured to you again." [8] King James expressed a current concept when he wrote, "The whole Scripture
. . . is composed of two parts, the Olde and new Testament.
The grounde of the former is the Law, which sheweth our sinne,
and containeth justice: the grounde of the other is Christ, who
pardoning sinne containeth grace." [9] Isabella's act of grace marks
her graduation from her nunnery to "that station in life to which
God had appointed her." She will make an excellent Duchess,
as the Duke will make her a good husband.

Isabella's silence at the end of the play has been much misunderstood. Even R. W. Chambers finds it ambiguous.[10] It is
dramatically necessary, since this is the end of the Duke's big
scene and attention must be focused on him. It is also appropriate to Elizabethan ideals of womanhood. However, as he
usually does, Shakespeare clearly indicates the required and
significant action which substitutes for, or interprets, speech.
When the hood which disguises Claudio is removed, the Duke
says to her:

> If he be like your brother, for his sake
> Is he pardoned, and for your lovely sake—
> Give me your hand and say you will be mine—
> He is my brother too. But fitter time for that.
> By this Lord Angelo perceives he's safe . . .
>
> (V, i, 486–90)

What should Isabella say? Whetstone gives his heroine some
inane "O's" and "Ah's" and "my brother's" to speak. Isabella's

action, implied in the Duke's speech, is more natural and more eloquent; stunned surprise, then a glad embrace of Claudio. The Duke is moved, but he cannot get her attention, even with a proposal of marriage. "Give me your hand and say you will be mine", he says, as he tries to draw her away, and then to join her, saying, "He is my brother, too." Then he gives up with "Fitter time for that," and turns to Angelo. Evidence that she has paid no attention to his marriage proposal in the joy of her reunion with her brother comes at the end of the scene when the Duke proposes again:

> Dear Isabel,
> I have a motion much imports your good, . . .

This line playfully echoes his first words to her in III, i, .154–56. There is, of course, a *double-entendre* in "motion," and as he completes the formula he no doubt takes her hand:

> Whereto if you'll a willing ear incline,
> What's mine is yours, and what is yours is mine.

Again Isabella does not need to speak. If she takes the Duke's hand, or allows him to take hers, this act, before witnesses, is a betrothal. To give her a speech at this point would be a violation of the tempo of the scene and of the concentration of the ending.

Such is Shakespeare's Isabella, and she takes her place naturally and with charm in the gallery of Shakespeare's heroines. In experience, if not in years, she is the youngest of them, with the possible exception of Miranda, and she is unique in that she is not in love and, although the best possible marriage is arranged as her reward, marriage is not her problem. Hers is a much heavier responsibility, and she does her best, under the guidance

and direction of Lucio, Angelo, Claudio, who each in his way
betrays her, and the Friar-Duke who works out her salvation
and claims her as his reward.

She is one of Shakespeare's most charming, and charmingly
feminine, women, not witty like Beatrice, nor adventurous like
Viola, and, in spite of her eloquence when prompted, inclined to
Cordelia's eloquent silences. The first mention of her comes from
Claudio and provides the key to the way in which the part
should be played,

> in her youth
> There is a prone and speechless dialect,
> Such as move men; . . .   (I, ii, 177–79)

It is her youth, not her chastity; her submissiveness, as well as
her eloquence, which charms and disarms, or should disarm, her
critics.

So much has been made of her decision to become a nun that
perhaps what Shakespeare says about it should be brought together. He makes it clear, at the beginning, that she has not
taken a nun's vows. Claudio says:

> This day my sister should the cloister enter,
> And there receive her approbation [that is,
>   begin her probation].   (I, ii, 172–73)

To emphasize her uncommitted state, in the first scene in which
she appears the nun says to her when Lucio knocks:

> Turn you the key, and know his business of him.
> You may, I may not; you are yet unsworn.
> When you have vowed, you must not speak with men
> But in the presence of the prioress . . .   (I, iv, 8–11)

She is "yet unsworn." [11]

There is still, perhaps, a question of how she should be dressed. On their first encounter, the Friar accosts her as "young sister" (III, i, 152), but since he has just overheard the dialogue between Isabella and Claudio, in which Claudio addresses her as "Sweet sister" (indicating their natural relationship), it is not clear that she is dressed as a nun. He calls her "the maid" when requesting the Provost to leave them alone together. On the other hand, a servant announces her to Angelo as "a sister," and, in the last act, when she is describing herself to the Duke, she says:

> I am the sister of one Claudio,
>
> .   .   .
>
> I, in probation of a sisterhood,
> Was sent to by my brother . . .   (V, i, 69–73)

It is true that in this scene she lies about her relations with Angelo, as she has been instructed to do, but otherwise she tells the truth. She is, then, at the very beginning of her novitiate, a period of testing to determine whether a girl has the "vocation" to become a nun. She is being instructed in the rules of the order. She should be wearing a simple, perhaps distinctive, dress or nunlike habit, but not the headdress which could not be put on until the head had been shaved as part of the ritual of taking final vows after a period of probation.[12] She is still free of choice as of action—as her action in going about unattended, and speaking alone with men, shows. If she had been a nun she could not have made her first decision as she did. She would not have been free to go to her brother in the first place—nor would Lucio have been allowed to speak to her. Her decision to become a nun has been exaggerated out of all proportion to the use Shake-speare makes of it. Perhaps that is what Professor Bullough means when he says, "She transcends the part she has henceforth to play." For those who prefer their own Isabella to Shakespeare's this may be true, but Shakespeare's most girlish heroine is a very different but more human and more consistent figure.

VI · The Duke

The change in the character and action of Isabella, from self-sacrificing heroine to innocent (and impotent) girl, made necessary a change in the part of the Duke. When she refuses to pay the monstrous ransom the action of the play has reached an impasse. If the ending is not to be tragic, either Angelo must relent, giving the play a weak and sentimental conclusion, or a superior force must be on the spot to restore a just order. Shakespeare chooses the second alternative, expanding the part of the just ruler, whom Cintio and Whetstone brought in at the end of the play to punish an unjust deputy. Of course, the author's creative process may have worked the other way. He may have decided to make a comedy out of the old melodrama by giving it a Harun al-Rashid Duke, and the reduction in the part of Isabella from heroine to helpless girl would have followed logically.

In any case, whatever the order of creation, the most important change in the plot, from both the structural and the ideological point of view, was the enlargement of the part of the Duke. He not only creates the situation by delegating his power and pretending to go abroad, but he also, while disguised and without recourse to power, by his cleverness saves both Isabella and Claudio; and then, after returning and resuming his power, he brings both Angelo and Isabella to repentance and metes out justice all around, not so much by the exercise of authority as by an elaborate and practical demonstration of wisdom and "craft."

Such a character must, by his unusual activities, appear somewhat mysterious. W. W. Lawrence regards him as "an essentially artificial figure elaborated to meet the requirements of the plot, and as a study in character, of minor importance in himself, or for the play." [1] Yet he recognizes that "Critics have frequently regarded him as the mainspring of the action, and his peculiar disposition as having profoundly influenced the development of the plot." This he considers "quite the reverse of the truth." However, once we recognize the elaborately artificial character of the whole comedy, it becomes possible to argue that both of these judgments are true. The Duke is both the mainspring of the action and an essentially and elaborately artificial figure whose peculiar disposition, if it does not profoundly influence the plot, does, nevertheless, color the whole play. In order to make this clear it is necessary to explore a further dimension of the play, the Duke as ruler.

It has long been recognized that the Duke bears some resemblance to King James. There are two allusions to a personal idiosyncrasy of his, dislike of the noise and· press of crowds.[2] One of these is voiced by the Duke, the other by Angelo. In the first scene the Duke says:

> I'll privily away; I love the people,
> But do not like to stage me to their eyes;
> Though it do well, I do not relish well
> Their loud applause and aves vehement,
> Nor do I think the man of safe discretion
> That does affect it.   (ll. 67–72)

The Duke is inviting comparison of himself with the King: he
has the same dislike of crowds; but he is not presuming to identify himself with, or impersonate, the King. Shakespeare must
have been careful to avoid any suggestion of impersonation. He
has reduced the rank of Whetstone's King of Hungary and Bohemia to that of a mere Duke of Vienna, and one who is abdicating, whereas King James had just ascended the throne. The
Duke's distaste for "loud applause and aves vehement" is a
compliment to the King's judgment, a gesture of fellow feeling
by which the Duke invites the King's sympathy and understanding; and, at the same time, it is a generalization which
establishes this attitude as one proper to rulers. King James's
impatience with, and dislike of, public appearances was in strong
contrast to Queen Elizabeth's love of them. As early as June 22,
1603, Mr. Thomas Wilson wrote to Sir Thomas Parry from
Greenwich about the King's incessant hunting, and he adds,
"The people . . . approve all their Prince's actions and words,
saving that they desyre some more of that generous affabilitye
wch ther good old Queen did afford them." [3] As early as 1586,
when he was twenty-one, a report of his disposition sent to Queen
Elizabeth described him as one who desired peace, loved hunting
and writing poetry, and loved solitude.[4] Just before the long-
delayed coronation procession, he undertook a private visit to
London to see the decorations, and was so frightened by the
crowd which formed to see him that he took refuge in the Royal
Exchange.[5] He hurried so fast through the Coronation Procession
of March 15, 1604, that "a great part" of the speeches "were left
unspoken." [6] "It is highness pleasure to be private," says Gilbert
Dugdale, reporting the King's displeasure at the crowds when he
visited the Royal Exchange.[7] Ben Jonson, in the "Panegyre"

(1604), in which he described the Coronation Procession, also excuses James for his impatience, saying:

> Mean while, the reuerend *Themis* drawes aside
> The Kings obeying will, from taking pride
> In these vaine stirres, and to his mind suggests
> How he may triumph in his subjects brests,
> With better pomp. . . .[8]

The second reference to a distaste for crowds comes from Angelo, the other ruler in the play, and so emphasizes the universality of the experience. Angelo is describing his emotions at the prospect of seeing Isabella again. He has a sense of suffocation:

> So play the foolish throngs with one that swounds,
> Come all to help him, and so stop the air
> By which he should revive; and even so
> The general, subject to a well-wished king,
> Quit their own part, and in obsequious fondness
> Crowd to his presence, where their untaught love
> Must needs appear offense.   (II, iv, 24–30)

The second simile is somewhat forced as an expression of Angelo's emotion; but it makes apology for the behavior of the English crowds who had so displeased King James, in the phrases, "a well-wished king . . . obsequious fondness . . . untaught love." In both references Shakespeare represents King James's dislike of crowds as normal to rulers.

The compliments to King James are not limited to these two passages, however. The whole character of Duke Vincentio was created not to represent, but to please and flatter, the King. For this purpose Shakespeare used the King's own picture of himself as it appears in his most successful and timely literary effort. The extensive use of the *Basilikon Doron: or His Maiesties Instructions to his Dearest Sonne Henrie the Prince* in *Measure for Measure* has been investigated, first by Dr. Louis Albrecht in 1914,[9] and then in a more scholarly way by Professor David L. Stevenson in 1959.[10] In rebuttal, alternative sources have been suggested for many of the principles expressed by the Duke; and the importance of the *Basilikon Doron* has been denied [11] because the enormous popularity of this little book in 1603 and 1604 has not been recognized, and its relation to the play has been treated from the point of view of source, rather than as material for familiar allusion. Dr. Albrecht does not discuss the popularity of the book, and Professor Stevenson was misled by the modern editor of it into believing that there were only four editions in 1603.[12] It has been treated as a source for ideas rather than as what it was, a basis for multiple allusions easily caught by a majority of the audience and so used as an important part of the comic effect.

The "king's book," as it was called, was published in Edinburgh in 1599. Then it was revised for English readers and secretly printed in London while Queen Elizabeth was dying. On March 28, four days after her death, and on the very day when the news was announced to King James in Edinburgh, John Norton, representing a syndicate of London stationers, entered the *Basilikon Doron* in the *Stationers' Register*; and on March 30, copies were bought in London.[13] Several presses were at work on it, but the supply could not keep up with the demand. The Stationers' Court fined the syndicate for having sold "great numbers" at more than the allowed price. On April 13, two weeks after its publication, Edward Allde was accused of having sold a pirated edition of 1,500 copies,[14] and before he submitted and paid his fine he printed and sold a second 1,500.

Copies of "several unrecorded editions by other printers" are extant, and ten or a dozen editions published by Norton in 1603 are known.[15]

Writing years after the event, Francis Bacon describes how the book prepared the way for King James's welcome to England: "falling into every man's hand [it] filled the whole realm as with a good perfume, or incense, before the King's coming in. For being excellently written, and having nothing of affectation, it did not only satisfy better than particular reports touching the King's disposition; but far exceeded any formal or curious edict or declaration which could have been devised of that nature, wherewith Princes in the beginning of their reigns do use to grace themselves, or at least express themselves graciously, in the eyes of their people." [16]

It was the most eagerly read book of the year. Orators and poets alike greeted the King with allusions, or more direct references, to it. Samuel Daniel published a "Panegyrike Congratulatorie" in which he praises the *Basilikon Doron*, beginning,

> We haue an euerlasting euidence
> Vnder thy hand, that now we need not dread
> Thou will be otherwise in thy designes
> Then there thou art in those iudiciall lines.   (st. 20)[17]

Although no one seems to have noticed it, Ben Jonson paraphrased it extensively in the first thirty-three lines of his "Panegyre" as Themis' speech to James, and then with a "he knew" he adds a further paraphrase.[18] William Camden, speaking of books published in support of King James's right to the English throne, adds, "But far beyond all these went the Book called BASILICON DORON, written by the King to his Son, wherein is most elegantly pourtrayed and set forth the Pattern of a most

excellent and every-way-accomplished Prince. Incredible it is how
many mens hearts and Affections he wone unto him by his writing of it, and what an Expectation of himself he raised amongst
all men, even to Admiration." [19] The lawyer and wit, Richard
Martin, in his *Speach* in the names of the Sheriffs of London
and Middlesex, welcoming James to London, says, "those excellent wholesome rules your Majestie will never transgresse, having
bound your Princely Sonne. . . ." Many similar references have
been gathered up by James Craigie[20] and by Professor Stevenson
from the orations of welcome, sermons, and pamphlets of the day.
In addition, both universities published volumes of student verse
commemorating the Queen's death and the King's accession, and
these too make reference to the King's book.[21]

It was the first English book to be immediately and widely
translated. John Florio turned it into Italian, John Pemberton
into Spanish. There were three French and two Dutch transla-
tions published in 1603, and it appeared in Latin, German, and
Welsh in 1604, and in Swedish in 1606.[22]

A Cambridge don, William Willymat, reduced its substance
to epigrams in Latin and English verse, "his Maiesties consent
and approbation being first had," and published his work as *A
Princes Looking Glasse* (Cambridge, 1603). So pleased was he
with "The late gracious acceptance . . . of that Princes Look-
ing-glasse" that he also published *A Loyal Subiects Looking-
Glasse*, in prose, which also draws heavily, and openly, on the
Basilikon Doron. Henry Peacham created a series of Latin emblems out of it, drawing the emblems himself and presenting the
illuminated manuscript to Prince Henry. In 1612 he published
an augmented version, turning the emblems into English.[23]

Aside from its timeliness, this little book has a great deal of literary interest. Addressed to Prince Henry, then only a child, it is written simply and with a great deal of charm. In his prefatory letter the King expresses the fear that he will not live to bring up his son, and this excuse introduces just the right note of sentiment for popular appeal. He also makes disarming admissions of his own mistakes, which he advises his son to avoid. And he expresses the highest ideals of royal absolutism.

In the 1603 edition he added an address to his readers, obviously aimed at his English audience, in which he says that this book "must be taken of all men, for the true image of my very mind, and forme of the rule, which I have prescribed to my selfe and mine." [24] How far his practice fell short of his avowed principles was not immediately apparent, although his extravagant claims to virtue must have hastened the disenchantment. It was not a blueprint of the new reign. But it was the pattern, and announced the key note, for all compliments intended to flatter King James. He himself referred to it frequently, as if it were an official statement of his policies.[25] It created the public image in which the King invited his subjects to see him, just as the "virgin Queen" had been Queen Elizabeth's public image, the formula for acceptable compliment. When, therefore, the Duke in *Measure for Measure* expresses, both in his actions and in his speeches, the same concepts of his duties and responsibilities which the King had expressed, there is no reason to doubt or question that Shakespeare was deliberately alluding to the King's book, the highly idealized, official portrait which everyone would recognize.

The *Basilikon Doron* is a short work, divided into three parts: "Of a Kings Christian dutie towards God," "Of a Kings Dutie in his office," and "Of a Kings Behavior in Indifferent Things."

Immediately following the title page, and preceding the letter to "Henry my Dearest Sonne" and the address to the Readers, is a sonnet entitled "The Argument," which epitomizes the point of view. It reads:

> God gives not Kings the stile of *Gods* in vaine,
> For on his throne his Scepter do they swey:
> And as their subjects ought them to obey,
> So Kings should feare and serue their God again.
> If then ye would enjoy a happie raigne,
> Obserue the statutes of your heauenly King,
> And from his Lawe, make all your Lawes to spring:
> Since his Lieutenant here ye should remaine,
> Reward the just, be stedfast, true, and plaine,
> Represse the proud, maintaining aye the right;
> Walke alwaies so, as ever in his sight,
> Who guards the godly, plaguing the prophane:
>   And so ye shall in Princely vertues shine,
>   Resembling right your mightie King Divine.

At the end of the third act in *Measure for Measure* the Duke steps out of his disguise and addresses the audience, like a chorus, to explain his principles of government and his plan for correcting Angelo. This soliloquy turns King James's concept of kingship into tetrameter verse:

> He who the sword of heauen will bear
> Should be as holy as severe;
> Pattern in himself to know,
> Grace to stand, and virtue go;
> More nor less to others paying
> Than by self-offenses weighing.
> Shame to him whose cruel striking
> Kills for faults of his own liking.

> Twice treble shame on Angelo,
> To weed my vice and let his grow.[26]

.   .   .

> Craft against vice I must apply;

and he goes on to explain, and justify, the substitution of Mariana for Isabella.

It is not that the ideas of princely duty expressed in this book are unusual. On the contrary, parallels to the Duke's utterances have been cited from Cicero, Erasmus, Sir Thomas Elyot, and even from Machiavelli. King James sprinkled his margins with citations of classical authorities.[27] What makes it so certain that Shakespeare was deliberately echoing the *Basilikon Doron* is that this is the book he could be sure his audience would recognize, and therefore allusions to it would be effective. In fact, in any picture of a "good" ruler created at this time, such recognition was to be expected, for it could not be avoided.

Professor Stevenson summarizes his findings by saying that the Duke "agreed with the new King not only in his dislike of the 'Aves' of the crowd, but also in his concept of virtue in action, his irritation at the 'unreverent speeches' of the common people, his insistence that the ruler should first subdue his own appetites before he attempted to subdue them in his subjects, and his wish to 'appear to the envious' in his 'own bringings-forth' both a scholar and a statesman." [28] Dr. Albrecht also supplies parallel passages (not always the same passages) for these points and quotes examples of King James's pride in his "statecraft" to illustrate the Duke's "Craft against vice I must apply" (III, ii, 260). He also puts forward the King's discussion of a ruler's marriage as a model for the proposal of the Duke to Isabella.[29]

Many parallel passages have been pointed out, and more can

be found, but it is not merely the echoes of the *Basilikon Doron,*
in the speeches, which are significant; but the fact that Shakespeare selected the most striking and obvious passages to echo,
passages which the most inattentive reader would remember.
And he modified the old plot by creating Lucio and Escalus, and
adapting Angelo, characters who illustrate elements in the King's
book. In addition to the choruslike speech at the end of Act III
which lightly echoes the King's introductory sonnet, the Duke's
soliloquy in IV, i echoes a conspicuous passage. Book III of the
Basilikon Doron opens with the statement, "It is a true olde
saying, That a King is as one set on a stage, whose smallest
actions and gestures, all the people gazinglie doe behold. . . ."
When he came to write "To the Reader" for the 1603 edition,
King James repeated this idea, almost verbatim, but with more
emphasis, adding "where all the beholders eyes are attentivelie
bent, to looke and pry in the least circumstance of their secretest
driftes . . ." [30] The Duke soliloquizes:

> O place and greatness, millions of false eyes
> Are stuck upon thee; volumes of report
> Run with these false and most contrarious quests
> Upon thy doings; thousand escapes of wit
> Make thee the father of their idle dream,
> And rack thee in their fancies.   (IV, i, 59–64)

Ben Jonson in his "Panegyre" follows the King's book more
literally, representing Themis as telling King James that

> Kings
> Are here on earth the most conspicuous things:
> That they, by Heaven, are plac'd vpon his throne,
> To rule like heauen; and haue no more, their owne,
> As they are men, then men. That all they doe,

> Though hid at home, abroad is search'd into:
> And being once found out, discouer'd lies
> Vnto as many enuies, there, as eyes.   (ll. 77–84)[31]

King James had suffered much abuse. According to his own
account, he had been misrepresented and misunderstood and his
writings misinterpreted. He had been the target of Jesuit defa-
mation as well as of Protestant abuse. A leader of the Scotch
Presbyterians had berated him to his face, and he says of this
sect, in the *Basilikon Doron,* "yee shall neuer finde with any
Hie-land or Border theeues greater ingratitude, and moe lies &
vile perjuries, then with these phanatike spirites." [32] Elsewhere
he speaks of "the malice of the children of enuie, who like waspes,
suckes venome out of euery wholesome hearbe." [33]

Henry Chettle bears witness in *Englandes Mourning Garment*
(1603) where his shepherd says, "my selfe haue seene & heard
with glowing eares some of them, euen in the fields of Calydon,
when his Excellence that is now our emperiall Shepheard, was
onely Lord of their foldes, speake of his Maiestie more auda-
ciously and malapertly, than any of us would doe of the meanest
officer." [34] One of the reasons given by King James for adding an
address "To the Reader" to his book is "by this preface, to cleere
such parts" of it as may be misrepresented.[35] He is especially
concerned with those who doubt the sincerity of his Protestantism because of his denunciation of the Puritans. But these
"breathing nothing but sedition and calumnies; aspiring without
measure, rayling without reason, and making their owne imaginations (without anie warrant of the worde) the square of their
conscience," [36] have aroused his just indignation. Indeed, "al
the common people [of Scotland] . . . judge and speake rashlie
of their Prince," but "I know no better meane, then so to rule,
as may iustlie stop their mouthes, from al such idle and vnreuerent

speeches." [37] He advises his son "so to temper and mixe your seueritie with mildnesse, that as the vniust railers may bee restrained with a reuerent awe; so the good. . . ." Again, in a passage in which he advises his son to "be well versed in authenticke histories," he warns him to suppress such "infamous invectives [against him] as Buchanan's and Knoxes Chronicles: . . . these infamous libels" and to "vse the law vpon the keepers thereof." [38]

Lucio, with his malicious and preposterous libeling of the Duke, epitomizes the King's detractors, though he does not *represent* them. He is neither a Jesuit nor a Puritan, but a libertine, and the vice of which he accuses the Duke is his own vice, not one of which the King was ever accused.[39]

Lucio has no counterpart in the old plot. He is a striking example of Shakespeare's cleverness and economy as a dramatist. In a sense he is the thread on which the action of the play is strung. He is described, in the cast of characters, as "a fantastic." He is very much a "humours" character, yet he plays two distinct and different parts: he is the sincere and devoted friend of Claudio who brings the reluctant Isabella to the rescue and coaches her in her plea for mercy for Claudio. Beginning in the latter part of Act III, however, Lucio is the persistent scandalizer and tormentor of the Duke: as he says to the Friar-Duke, "I am a kind of burr; I shall stick." [40] What keeps him from inconsistency is his concern for Claudio. As is common with his kind of libertine, he is a sentimentalist. He thinks that Isabella is "a thing enskied and sainted" (I, iv, 34), because she is about to enter a nunnery, yet he has no hesitation about making use of her to help Claudio; and when Isabella arrives in her pleading with Angelo at "Hark how I'll bribe you," Lucio, like Angelo, is suddenly interested. He comments, "You had marred all else"

(II, ii, 148), but Isabella in her girlish innocence prates on about "fasting maids" praying "ere sunrise," and Angelo, with something more immediate to think about, replies, "Well, come to me tomorrow." Lucio seizes the opportunity to get her away.

This is all very loyal to his friend Claudio, but when we meet him again in Act III, scene ii, ll. 41 ff., he is turning a very cold shoulder with derisive comments on poor Pompey, who has greeted him as "a gentleman and a friend of mine." He is a fair-weather friend to Pompey, not involving himself in Pompey's trouble. Yet it comes out that his false report of the Duke's vices is motivated by resentment of the Duke's absence: "It was a mad fantastical trick of him to steal from the state." And when the Friar-Duke, in a huff, asks his name and threatens to report him, he shows what is in his mind by saying, "But no more of this; canst thou tell if Claudio die tomorrow or no?" (III, ii, 158–59) Lucio's next speech is a wonderful study of emotional thinking. His impotent rage lashes out at the Duke and Angelo alternately; the Friar has replied, "Why should he die, sir?" and Lucio answers crudely and petulantly:

Why? For filling a bottle with a tun-dish. I would the Duke we talk of were returned again; this ungenitured agent will unpeople the province with continency. Sparrows must not build in his house-eaves because they are lecherous. The Duke yet would have dark deeds darkly answered; he would never bring them to light; would he were returned. Marry, this Claudio is condemned for untrussing. Farewell, good friar; I prethee, pray for me. The Duke, I say again, would eat mutton on Fridays. He's not past it yet, and I say to thee, he would mouth with a beggar, though she smelt brown bread and garlic. Say that I said so; farewell. (ll. 161–72)

The Friar-Duke's comment on this outburst echoes the King's feelings:

No might nor greatness in mortality
Can censure 'scape; back-wounding calumny
The whitest virtue strikes. What king so strong
Can tie the gall up in the slanderous tongue?

When Lucio next appears, at the end of Act IV, scene iii, he is lamenting, in his own way, the death (as he supposes) of his friend: "O pretty Isabella, I am pale at mine heart to see thine eyes so red; thou must be patient. I am fain to dine and sup with water and bran; I dare not for my head fill my belly; one fruitful meal would set me to't" (that is, make me incur the penalty Claudio has suffered). And again his resentment at the absence of the Duke breaks out: "But they say the Duke will be here tomorrow. By my troth, Isabel, I loved thy brother; if the old fantastical Duke of dark corners had been at home, he had lived." (ll. 149-55)

Finally, when he erupts in Act V, l. 74, to plague the Duke with interruptions for the rest of this long scene, it is because he is anxious to be credited with his effort to save Claudio. Later in the scene (ll. 127 ff.), he interrupts again to accuse the Friar of the scandalmongering against the Duke which he himself has been guilty of. The situation is hilariously funny to the audience, but it is also psychologically accurate for this sentimentalist-libertine. Most of us have suffered from being reported to have said what, in fact, our accuser has said to us, often a censure which we rejected at the time. Lucio simply has one of those convenient memories which operates always to his own advantage. His abuse of the supposedly absent Duke is apt because it characterizes not the Duke, but Lucio and the kind of people who abuse their ruler.

It has been suggested that Lucio had recognized the Duke in his disguise but this is surely a mistake. Some of his remarks are

more true than he knows, and that is a source of amusement to
the audience, but he would hardly have admitted to the Friar
that he was the father of Kate Keepdown's child if he had had
any inkling of the fact that the Friar was the Duke in disguise.
And his final blunder of abusing the Friar to the Duke is inex-
plicable on that basis.

His tormenting of the Duke with these false reports is, however, both comic and appropriate if we recognize the occasion for
the play, the entertainment of King James and the running
allusions to the "King's book." Shakespeare is tactful in keeping
his parallels at a distance from reality. Lucio is a "fantastic," a
light fellow, more a Sir Pecksall Brockas[41] than a Puritan.
Lucio's accusations against the Duke were the opposite of the
truth. So far as women were concerned King James was, and was
reported to be, a model of virtue. He told his son that he would
leave no bastards to plague him, as King James had been plagued
by his father's and his grandfather's. He even invited comparison
with Queen Elizabeth in chastity, with the difference that he had
provided his subjects with an heir to the throne, and she had
not.[42] Shakespeare has kept safely away from the King's person,
in representing the Duke as abused by false report. While appeal-
ing to the King's experience with slanderers, thereby invoking
his sympathy, he has avoided the indiscretion of personal allusion.

The character of Angelo also draws something from the King's
book, which devotes several pages to the difference between a
king and a tyrant. "The one acknowledgeth himselfe ordained
for his people, having received from God a burden of gouern-
ment whereof he must be count-able: the other thinketh his
people ordained for him, a prey to his passions and inordinate
appetites, . . ." Moreover, the tyrant, "counterfeiting the Sainte
while he once creepe in credit, will then (by inverting all good

lawes to serve only for his unruly priuate affections) frame the Common-weale ever to advance his particular. . . ." [43] This is exactly what Angelo does when he orders the execution of Claudio, not to serve the ends of justice but to protect himself. The King concludes this section: "I shew how a Tyrant would enter like a Saint while hee found himself fast under-foote, and then would suffer his unruly affections to burst foorth. Therefore be yee contrarie, . . . to that Quinquennium Neronis," etc. Be firm at the beginning.[44] This is the pattern set by Angelo, and the King's repeated reference to "a Saint" may have suggested the name *Angelo* for this tyrant of the King's creation.

While the King advises his son to be firm at the beginning, he laments that he, himself, had not been so:

For if otherwise yee kyth your clemencie at the first, the offences would soon come to such heapes, and the contempt of you growe so great, that when yee would fall to punish, the number of them to be punished would exceede the innocent; and ye would be troubled to resolve whome-at to beginne: and against your nature would bee compelled then to wracke many, whom the chastisement of a few in the beginning might have preserved. But in this, my over-deare bought experience may serue you for a sufficient lesson. For I confesse, where I thought (by being gracious at the beginning) to winne all mens hearts to a louing and willing obedience, I by the contrarie found, the disorder of the countrie, and the losse of my thanks to be all my reward.[45]

It is just this experience which, as the Duke explains to Friar Thomas, has motivated his abdication. Like King James, he has

> ever loved the life removed
> And held in idle price to haunt assemblies
> Where youth and cost witless bravery keeps.   (I, iii, 8–10)

And he has neglected to enforce the laws strictly:

> We have strict statutes and most biting laws,
> The needful bits and curbs to headstrong wills,
> Which for this fourteen years we have let slip;
>
> .   .   .
>
> in time the rod
> Becomes more mocked than feared; so our decrees,
> Dead to infliction, to themselves are dead,
> And Liberty plucks Justice by the nose;   (ll. 19–29)

but he dare not "unloose this tied-up justice" himself.

> Sith 'twas my fault to give the people scope,
> 'Twould be my tyranny to strike and gall them
> For what I bid them do: for we bid this be done
> When evil deeds have their permissive pass
> And not the punishment.   (ll. 35–39)

And so he has appointed Angelo to rule while he, disguised as a friar, will "Visit both prince and people."

Two further elements in this play require comment: the religious activities and the device of a disguised monarch. King James's concept of God-appointed kingship, expressed in the sonnet I have quoted, and in the first book of the *Basilikon Doron*, gives ample warrant for the Duke's disguise as a friar and his activities as a representative of God. James advises his son to treat his subjects "as their naturall father and kindly maister," [46] to "be called a loving nourish-Father to the Church," [47] and "since yee must be *communis parens* to al your people, so choose your seruantes," etc. [48] His basic concept is that the king is God's representative on earth. He is answerable to God for his conduct, and so has a double obligation, to God and to his people. He says, "teach your people by your example," [49] both by

abstaining from evil and by doing good. Just so the Duke advises
Angelo on the need to *use* his virtue:

> Thyself and thy belongings
> Are not thine own so proper, as to waste
> Thyself upon thy virtues, they on thee.

> .   .   .

> for if our virtues
> Did not go forth of us, 'twere all alike
> As if we had them not. Spirits are not finely touched
> But to fine issues, nor Nature never lends
> The smallest scruple of her excellence
> But like a thrifty goddess she determines
> Herself the glory of a creditor,
> Both thanks and use.   (I, i, 29–40)

King James wrote: "neither think it enough to abstaine from euill,
and do no good: nor thinke not that if ye doe manie good
things, it may serue you for a cloake to mixe euil turnes there-
with." [50] Elsewhere he says, citing Aristotle and Cicero: "For
it is not enough that yee haue and retaine (as prisoners) within
your selfe neuer so manie good qualities and vertues, except ye
emploie them, and set them on worke, for the weale of them
that are committed to your charge: Virtutis enim laus omnis in
actione consistit." [51] The Duke's activity in watching his deputy,
and in haunting the prison, even in giving spiritual advice to
those in need of it, is in keeping with the King's concept of his
duties. He tells his son to "delight to haunt your Session" (a
duty in which Angelo so egregiously fails), "wearie not to heare
the complaints of the oppressed." [52]

The device of a monarch-in-disguise may, as I have already
suggested, have been the basic change in the old plot from which
all the other changes flowed. From the time of Harun al-Rashid

onward, tales of rulers going about in disguise have appealed to
the popular imagination. In the Renaissance a group of such tales
gathered about the name of the Roman emperor, Alexander
Severus. Sir Thomas Elyot's use of this figure to illustrate the
duties of a good ruler has been put forward as the source of
Shakespeare's Duke,[53] but there was such a figure much closer
to King James.

For the English in 1603 the question even before "What is the
Scotch King like?" would naturally be "What is his title to the
English throne?" King James inherited that title from his grand-
father, James V, son of James IV of Scotland who married
Margaret, daughter of Henry VII and sister of Henry VIII of
England. James V had been as popular and romantic a figure in
Scotland as Henry V had been in England and, like Henry V,
he had died young. He had come to the throne as an infant, as
had his namesake and grandson, King James VI of Scotland and
I of England, and the troubles of King James's youth were very
like those of his grandfather. James V was famous for going
among his people incognito as the "Goodman of Ballengiech,"
and he went abroad in disguise to make a romantic love-match
with Madeleine, elder daughter of Francis I of France.[54] It may
have been this episode in family history which inspired Charles
I's wooing of the Infanta of Spain; as the *Basilikon Doron,* by
its phenomenal success, no doubt inspired the production of that
pitiful failure, the *Ikon Basilikon.*

King James VI of Scotland, and I of England, was proud of
his grandfather, and especially of his popularity as "the poor
man's king," as he called him.[55] Because of his own weak legs
and timid nature, King James could not undertake any such
adventures, although his interminable hunting (on horseback),
and the informalities of the hunting lodge, may have been a kind

of substitute. At any rate, in spite of the troublesome bastards, whose existence James VI deplored, James V was a romantic and popular figure, the source of the Scotch claim to the English throne; and his adventures incognito may have suggested the Duke's, serving as another channel for the gratulation of the King which was the wellspring of this play.

Shakespeare had already written a play about Henry V of England, who also was a relative of King James, and it is perhaps worth noting that *Henry V* was acted before the King during the same holiday season as *Measure for Measure*. It will be recalled that Shakespeare's Henry V also wooed a French princess for love, and that the English king went among his soldiers incognito on the eve of battle. King James could take pride in his kinship with both of the hero kings. His kinship with Henry V was inherited from both his grandfather and his grandmother. When James IV and Margaret Tudor were married in 1503 (just a hundred years before their great-grandson inherited the English throne), they had to get a papal dispensation because both were descended from John Beaufort, half brother of Henry IV of England. So the King stayed his hunting to see *Henry V* on January 7, 1605. Shakespeare's interest in the ancestors of King James was shortly to provide the story for *Macbeth*.[56]

Other elements in the Duke's similarity to King James have been commented on by Professor Stevenson: his love of intrigue, his clemency, and his pride in his scholarship. King James's love of stratagems is illustrated by his behavior in dealing with the culprits in the "By-plot." He signed the warrants for the execution of Lord Cobham, Lord Grey, and Sir Griffin Markeham, but he also signed countermands of these orders, instructing the sheriff not to deliver the countermands until the three men had confessed on the scaffold and were at the very point of being

executed. As Sir Dudley Carleton described the scene, it must
have been as obviously dramatic as the last act of *Measure for
Measure*.[57] Similar episodes show the King's fondness for dramatics. His account of the Gowrie affair (the only one we have)
reads like something out of *The Castle of Otranto*. Shakespeare
was familiar with the alleged Gowrie conspiracy, because his
company produced a play about it in the late summer of 1604.[58]

King James prided himself on his "kingcraft." He tells his son:
"above all virtues, studie to knowe well your owne craft, which
is to rule your people," [59] and ends his book with the words,
"And being content to let others excell in other things, let it be
your chiefest earthlie glorie, to excell in your own craft." [60]

Statecraft is still a respectable epithet, but the King's love of
stratagems, of devious courses, brought the less reputable meaning
of *craft* into play also. The word is used with perfect ambiguity
when the Duke says:

> Craft against vice I must apply;
> With Angelo tonight shall lie
> His old betrothèd, but despisèd;
> So disguise shall by th'disguisèd
> Pay with falsehood, false exacting,
> And perform an old contracting.   (III, ii, 260–65)

Indeed, the Duke "like power divine" manages his subjects skillfully, even before the last act, using strategies rather than authority to achieve ends which are not clear until they have been
fully accomplished—using pretenses, deceptions, and simple lies
freely to achieve what we must recognize are, in the idiom of
their day, the best of moral ends.

If there is much that seems to us questionable in the behavior
of the Duke, his general clemency is in accordance with the

King's exalted concept of his office. He advises his heir, "vse Justice, but with such moderation, as it turne not in tyrannie," explaining, "For lawes are ordained as rules of vertuous & sociall liuing, & not to be snares to trap your good subjects: and therefore the law must be interpreted according to the meaning, and not to the literal sense thereof: *nam ratio est anima legis.*" [61] This is the principle of the Duke, and, on the working level, of Escalus in the trial scene, but it is entirely neglected by Angelo in his dealing with Claudio and in the matter of Elbow's charges against Froth. Escalus is a model of the just and wise magistrate whose conduct provides pointed contrast to Angelo's. The King, while advising his son to "haunt your Session," nevertheless instructs him, "Remit euery thing to the ordinarie judicature, for eschewing of confusion: but let it be your own craft, to take a sharpe account of euerie man in his office." [62] Accordingly, the Duke promises the patient and wise Escalus his due reward, while he grants justice, tempered with mercy, to Angelo. By his "craft" he has prevented the worst of these crimes, and so does not need to punish with severity.

King James, in setting a high standard of studiousness for his son, was conforming to the Renaissance ideal of the education of the prince, but he was most vain of his own scholarship.[63] He advises his son to read the Bible diligently,[64] to know his subjects, especially their vices, to visit parts of the country, and to know "the forme of making warres," [65] as well as to know the laws and the chronicles and a "reasonable" amount of the arts and sciences.[66] When, therefore, Lucio describes the Duke to the Friar (that is, to his face) as "A very superficial, ignorant, unweighing fellow," and the Friar defends him (that is, himself) indignantly: "Let him be but testimonied in his own bringings-forth, and he shall appear to the envious a scholar, a statesman, and a soldier" (III, ii, 135-37), the situation is humorous on several levels. Since the audience knows that the Friar is the Duke in disguise, it is amusing that the Duke should be forced to defend himself, but his words are also a sly compliment to King James because the Duke exemplifies the King's avowed principles. Yet it is kept general by its use of the conventional Renaissance trio of "scholar, statesman, soldier." The last, King James certainly was not, yet as a monarch he must be versed in warfare, as he advises his son. The use of the term "bringings-forth" is amusingly ambiguous, since it could refer either to writings (and King James was inordinately proud of his) or to acts of government. And, of course, Lucio's blunder in speaking ill of the Duke to his face is amusing to begin with.

Like King James, the Duke is sensitive, and later in this same scene he asks Escalus, "of what disposition was the Duke?" to which Escalus responds with the highest praise, "One that, above all other strifes, contended especially to know himself." "What pleasure was he given to?" Escalus replies, "Rather rejoicing to see another merry, than merry at anything which professed to make him rejoice: a gentleman of all temperance." (III, ii, 217-23) Again we recognize both the Renaissance ideal, and King James's claim. He assured his son that moderation is the chief of the four cardinal virtues, and is to be applied to justice as to all the others.[67]

As Professor Stevenson says, we are "forced to conclude that Shakespeare's intensions were fairly deliberate, that he created in the Duke a character whose acts and whose theories of government would be interesting to the new age and its new King because they were so carefully like ones which the King had identified as his own." [68] In fact, since it must be assumed that the audience was already familiar with the *Basilikon Doron*, the burden of proof rests on anyone who denies that Shakespeare was deliberately alluding to it; and that he turned the old tragicomic plot into pure comedy by means of it; using it to establish the "good" character of the Duke in the first act, in his talks, first with Escalus, and then with Angelo, and finally, in scene iii, with Friar Thomas. Then in Act II we see him attending to the spiritual needs of Juliet (scene iii), and in the opening of Act III giving "philosophical" advice to Claudio. By this time the audience should be confident that the Duke will manage to save Claudio. Otherwise the irony and paradox of his advice to "Be absolute for death" would seem too harsh. His arrangement to overhear the conference between Claudio and Isabella has the effect of tantalizing the audience—why doesn't he *do* something? what *will* he do? And the suspense is immediately resolved by his conference with Isabella.

We are reassured by the presence of the Duke in the prison even more fully than we are by the presence of the constables and the arrest of Borachio in *Much Ado About Nothing*. In both plays there is a hitch. Justice seems to have failed. Leonato is in a hurry and refuses to hear Dogberry's windy report. Angelo breaks his word to Isabella and orders Claudio's execution. But the Duke is a much greater reassurance to the audience than is Dogberry that this is all going to work out satisfactorily. In case there should be any doubt, he steps out of his disguise at the end of Act III to say plainly what his principles are and what he intends to do.

It is not so much that the Duke is an "artificial figure elaborated to meet the requirements of the plot," as that the plot has been adapted to fit the character of the Duke. And the Duke is "the mainspring of the action," [69] although he is a composite of ideals most artificially combined.

King James must, surely, have been delighted with this stage Duke. A recent historian says of him, "he was constantly dreaming of making the world over through his intrigues and stratagems." "His favorite sport, next to hunting, was diplomacy." [70] In discussing this play, Charles Knight, in the nineteenth century, agreed with George Chalmers, in the eighteenth, that the Duke was very like King James: "there is the same desire in each to get behind the curtain and pull the strings which move the puppets." [71]

The whole play works so admirably for the gratification of King James, not only in its echoes of the King's own "bringings-forth," in the Duke and Angelo and Lucio, in the action as in the speeches, that it seems reasonably obvious that it was planned and written for the occasion. That does not mean that it was merely an ephemeral piece, like a Christmas pantomime. In the first place, plays were not "opened" or tried out at court.[72] They were performed first in the regular playing place of the company, that is, at the Globe on the Bankside, where they were seen by all and sundry, both high and low. If a play was not liked by its popular audience, as in the case, for example, of Jonson's *Sejanus,* it could hardly be considered for a court performance, although, in the case of *Sejanus,* the play was also objected to by members of the King's council, and so it was doubly damned.[73] It seems evident that those who selected plays for the royal entertainment attended public performances, so that success on the public stage was a *sine qua non* of a court performance. Evidence of the great popularity of the *Basilikon Doron* is important, therefore, as showing that not only at court, but also in the public theater, and even among the groundlings, this play, with its Duke modeled from "the King's book," was rich in a topicality which everyone could enjoy, because everyone was familiar with the contents of the *Basilikon Doron*. It is a Christmas play, but we do not have to wait until Twelfth-night to enjoy the play of that name, nor until midsummer's night for that one. We need not doubt that in its day it was by no means the least popular of Shakespeare's comedies. It was great theater, an incomparably witty play, an actor's play, par excellence, and there are aspects of it which remain to be explored.

VII · The King and the King's Players

One of the most amazing and puzzling achievements of this play is the echoing of the King's expressed principles of rule, and even allusion to a personal weakness of his, without suggesting impersonation, since that would certainly have given offense. Reducing the rank of the play's ruler, from King or Emperor to Duke, was a precaution. Vincentio is a ruler of whom King James could not fail to approve, since he so closely modeled himself on the King's book, "the true image of my very mind, and form of rule";[1] but the King was the Duke's superior in rank and (at least in his own estimation) in "kingcraft." The Duke is put to desperate shifts to bring about the happy denouement. He produces Mariana and arranges for the safety of both Isabella and Claudio; and then, while he boasts to the Provost that Claudio's "countermand" will surely come, the message arrives: "Let Claudio be executed by four of the clock; and in the afternoon, Barnardine." He quickly seizes on Barnardine as a possible substitute for Claudio, but the Provost has sworn to obey the Duke or his deputy, and so the disguised Duke has to produce "the hand and seal of the Duke" and promise his return "within these two days," in order to secure the Provost's cooperation. Then

Barnardine refuses to be executed, and a second substitute must be found. Throughout Act IV the Duke is hard put to it to save Claudio. He is no King of unlimited power, but only a poor Duke who lives by his wits, so to speak.

The person of the Duke and his manner of speech should not, and need not, in any way echo the person and speech of the King. In fact, in his first speech, the Duke sounds very like Polonius. Later he sounds like Hamlet's uncle. Even when he is echoing the *Basilikon Doron* there is no hint of paraphrase or parody of the style. The Duke begins pompously:

> Of government the properties to unfold,
> Would seem in me t'affect speech and discourse. (I, i, 3–4)

We are reminded of the equally pompous vacuity of

> to expostulate
> What majesty should be, what duty is,
> Why day is day, night night, and time is time,
> Were nothing but to waste night, day, and time.
>> (*Hamlet*, II, ii, 86–89)

When he addresses Isabella for the first time, his sugared diction is rhetoric in another key:

The hand that hath made you fair hath made you good. The goodness that is cheap in beauty makes beauty brief in goodness; but grace, being the soul of your complexion, shall keep the body of it ever fair. (III, i, 179–82)

In III, ii, 209–15, he indulges in what he himself calls a riddle. In IV, ii, 104–9, we have a series of gnomic couplets; and in III, ii, 244–65, he speaks in tetrameters whose artificial and tripping rhythm is in strong contrast to the King's style either in prose or verse. In fact he talks in a gallimaufry of styles as if deliberately exhibiting virtuosity. His lines on the miseries of life (III, i, 5–41) are a set speech, like Polonius' advice to Laertes,[2] or Jacques' "All the world's a stage";[3] and yet when he has business to transact, as when he castigates Pompey, he can be direct and succinct enough:

> Fie, sirrah, a bawd, a wicked bawd!
> The evil that thou causest to be done,
> That is thy means to live. . . .   (III, ii, 17 ff.)

Finally, in the fifth act, when he manages and dominates the whole long scene, he speaks briefly and develops a distinctive style which is remarkable for its force and effectiveness.

This verbal virtuosity of the Duke's is partly cause and partly result of the mysteriousness of his character. He talks in many veins and manages to keep his audience, both on stage and off, guessing. His variousness makes him an "artificial figure" as W. W. Lawrence observed, even while he is the mainspring of the whole. But the variety of his manners of speech gives his personality a mystery and vagueness which help to dissociate the Duke from the personality of King James.

The danger and folly of attempting to represent the monarch on the stage is well and briefly illustrated by John Chamberlain's report of a tragedy which the King's Men had prepared for this same Christmas season. In a letter dated December 18, 1604, Chamberlain wrote, "the tragedie of Gowrie with all the action and actors hath ben twise represented by the Kings players, with exceding concourse of all sortes of people, but whether the matter or manner be not well handled, or that yt be thought unfit that princes should be plaide on the stage in theyre life time, I heare that some great counsaillors are much displeased with yt: and so is thought shalbe forbidden."[4] Here we have a concise picture of the preparation and censorship of plays, such as *Measure for Measure* must also have undergone. It was not merely a matter of an official reading of the script; nor was it enough that it should please the multitude. A play was given a showing before all sorts of people including, evidently, the King's "great counsaillors." The "tragedie of Gowrie" must have been an attempt to dramatize the "Gowrie conspiracy" of 1600, which the King claimed had been an attempt on his life, and his escape from which he celebrated yearly thereafter on August 5. The play on this subject was probably forbidden since nothing more is recorded of it. Which of the two alternatives suggested by Chamberlain was the cause of the censorship we cannot know; probably both.[5]

The Privy Council would naturally be especially careful at the beginning of a new reign to check any plays with topical implications. Samuel Daniel was in serious trouble over his *Philotas* in 1604,[6] because this tragedy, while purporting to be about ancient history, rather obviously reflects the fall of the Earl of Essex in 1601. The Earl was dead, but King James had promptly pardoned all those still living who had been Essex' followers, and Daniel denied the allusion, claiming that he had written the first three acts of *Philotas* before Essex' fall. Somewhat the same fate which befell the tragedy of *Gowrie* befell Jonson's *Sejanus* also, about this time. Many years later Jonson told William Drummond of Hawthornden that "he was called befor ye Councel for his Sejanus & accused both of popperie & treason."[7] Since the theme of *Sejanus* (also ostensibly a history play) is the danger of a monarch's entertaining favorites and flatterers and devoting himself to pleasure while others ruled for him, its topical applicability to King James is sufficiently obvious,[8] although Jonson, of course, denied it.[9] Apparently about this time, also, Jonson and Chapman were imprisoned for writing *Eastward Ho,* and in some danger of having their noses slit.[10] The wise and prudent Shakespeare, meanwhile, was serenely writing *Othello,* produced at court on November 1, 1604.[11] There was no discernible topicality in that tragedy, and obviously there was nothing that would offend the King in *Measure for Measure,* although there was a great deal that was topical in it. There were the allusions to Jonson's *Masque of Blackness,* and to the Duke of Holstein's Hungarian undertaking, to the King's dislike of crowds, and to his *Basilikon Doron,* as well as to the Christmas occasion. But the purpose of the play, to flatter, entertain, and please the King was kept firmly in mind. Shakespeare did not attempt to advise or instruct him. On the contrary, he took instruction from him.

There was, however, a further purpose which is evident in the play, and that was to recommend the King's players to him, to show off the skills of the playwright and his company. Because of the plague which closed the London theaters from the beginning of the reign until April of 1604, there had been very little opportunity to produce new plays. The King had remained away from London during the Christmas season of 1603/4, and while his players were paid for eight plays during this season, there is no reason to suppose that any of them were new.[12] Moreover, the King's Men were faced with stiff competition. Both the Queen and Prince Henry had taken troops of actors into their service. The Queen's was a company of boys, but the Prince's Men were led by the redoubtable Ned Allen and in the season under discussion they gave Shakespeare's company stiff competition. Beginning on November 1, the King's Men produced *Othello* at court. On the 4th they produced *The Merry Wives of Windsor* there, but on November 23 and 24, and again on December 14 and 19, the Prince's troup entertained the court. The King's Men had a second inning with *Measure for Measure* on the 26th and the *Comedy of Errors* on the 28th. On the 27th there was a mask for the wedding of Philip Herbert, soon to be Earl of Montgomery, and Robert Cecil's niece, the Lady Susan Vere. The Queen's Revels performed on December 30 and January 1 and 3, and Jonson's *Masque of Blackness* was presented on the 6th (Twelfth Night). The King's Men gave *Henry V* on the 7th and *Every Man Out of His Humour* on the 8th. Then the King went hunting, but the Queen and most of the court saw *Love's Labour's Lost* at the Earl of Southampton's house between the 9th and the 12th.[13] The Prince's players acted at court on January 15 and 22, and the King's Men played *Every Man in His Humour* on February 2. They also had a play ready for the 3d, but it was not called for. On the 5th the Prince's troup played again, but on the 10th the King saw *The Merchant of Venice* and was so pleased with it that he asked to see it again on the 12th. Meanwhile, on the 11th, they acted *The Spanish Maze*. The Prince's troup played at court again on the 19th and ended the season.[14] Altogether we have record of twenty-three plays and two masks between November 1 and the beginning of Lent (February 20), of which the King's Men produced eleven, and eight of these were Shakespeare's. Two were Jonson's.

This program tells us several things: for one, the Prince's troup under Ned Allen presented very strong competition, although the Queen's boy actors had choice dates at what was normally the climax of the season.[15] For another thing, Ben Jonson was suddenly an important figure. He had caught the Queen's fancy with his masks,[16] and the failure of *Sejanus* had not hurt him at court. He had found his forte, not in instructive tragedy nor in satiric comedy, but in extravagant flattery and show. The first of the famous and lavishly expensive masks (the King paid ten pounds for a play; this mask cost over three thousand pounds), in the production of which he collaborated with the architect, Inigo Jones, was performed by the Queen and her ladies on Twelfth Night of this Christmas season. Shakespeare's company revived Jonson's two *Everyman* comedies to catch some of his glory, but Shakespeare must have felt the need to bestir himself to compete with this rising star.

The list of Shakespeare's plays produced during this season is surprising for its revival of early work. His *Comedy of Errors* was revived, apparently without much change;[17] and *Love's Labour's Lost* was prepared, and when it was not needed to entertain the King, Burbage persuaded the chamberlain of the Earl of Southampton that it was suitable for the Queen's entertainment at Southampton House.[18] These revivals may have been in response to the King's taste for classical form and subject matter, and for short plays, but it seems probable that he had already seen most of Shakespeare's plays then in existence. Two bits of evidence point in this direction. In this season he saw the last two Falstaff plays. Surely we can assume that he had already seen the first two, although there is no record of it. During the Christmas of 1603/4 he paid for eight plays in addition to one produced while he was visiting Wilton on December 2, which tradition makes *As You Like It*.[19] Of these eight, one was the *Fair Maid of Bristow* and one was a play of Robin Goodfellow, usually identified as *A Midsummer Night's Dream*. Whether the other six were all Shakespeare's, we do not know, but the record of arrangement for a performance of *Love's Labour's Lost* for the entertainment of the Queen and her guest at Southampton House in January, 1605, tells us two further things. When Sir Walter Cope, the Earl of Southampton's chamberlain, was

arranging that entertainment, Burbage came at his summons "&
sayes ther ys no new playe that the quene hath not seene, but
they have Revyved an olde one, . . ." [20] When had she seen
Twelfth Night, or *Much Ado About Nothing?* The court must
have seen the latter fairly recently, since it was expected to enjoy
echoes of that play, and especially of Dogberry, in *Measure for
Measure.* Yet there is no record of payment for these plays by
King James, unless they are among the six presented during the
Christmas of 1603/4, and not now identifiable. Perhaps there
were plays at Somerset House in the Strand in August when the
Spanish Ambassador was entertained extravagantly there and the
King's Men were paid for being in attendance. But the record
of the Queen's entertainment by the Earl of Southampton should
remind us that the King was often a guest also, and that he
probably did not pay for all of the plays put on for his amusement. The records we have show only payments by the royal
exchequer, but the King's Men could be hired by others. [21] For
example, when Burbage had completed the arrangements for
entertaining the Queen at Southampton House with *Love's
Labour's Lost,* we know that he went next to the house of Robert
Cecil, recently created Lord Cranbourne, who was preparing to
entertain the Queen two days after her visit to Southampton
House. He carried a message from one chamberlain to the other,
"Ready attending your pleasure." Certainly Cecil was under
obligation to equal or outdo Southampton's entertainment, and
the attendance of Burbage suggests that Cecil also may have
engaged the King's Men to put on a play.

The program of plays for the holidays of 1604/5 is one of only
two preserved, and its authenticity has been accepted so recently
that we have not yet taken full account of what it can tell us of
the theater in general, and of Shakespeare's fortunes in particu-

lar; but it is obvious that King James found Shakespeare's comic vein much to his liking, and we can learn from *Measure for Measure* something about the plays he had seen and the kind of comedy he liked. The play also shows the dramatist exhibiting his skill, and providing lines which will enable the actors to exhibit theirs, and even to allude to other parts they have played, as he alludes to other plays he has written.

The most obvious and extensive of these allusive echoes is the reincarnation of Constable Dogberry as Constable Elbow. Not only is the whole scene of the trial reminiscent of the hearing Dogberry attempted to conduct in *Much Ado About Nothing,* but there are other echoes of situation and even verbal allusions which suggest that the play had been especially well received by the King and his court recently enough to be well remembered. Perhaps it had been part of the entertainment provided at one of the noble houses visited by King James during the royal progress of the summer of 1604, or, as I have already suggested, perhaps it was put on at Somerset House in August as part of the lavish entertainment which accompanied the signing of the treaty of peace with Spain.

In the trial scene in *Measure for Measure* Elbow talks like Dogberry, and Pompey, although he takes the part of Verges in the dialogue, also echoes Dogberry. Indeed, some of Dogberry's tediousness is transferred to him. There seems to be a verbal allusion when Escalus says to Pompey, "Come, you are a tedious fool; to the purpose" (II, i, 110). Leonato had said to Dogberry and Verges, "Neighbors, you are tedious," and Dogberry had replied, "It pleases your worship to say so, but we are the poor duke's officers; but truly, for mine own part, if I were as tedious as a king, I could find in my heart to bestow it all of your worship" (III, v, 17–21). However, Pompey's tedious account of the dish of stewed prunes is not like Dogberry's inability to tell Leonato about the "two auspicious persons" whom the watch has "comprehended." Pompey's purpose is entirely different, for, while Dogberry intends but fails to communicate, Pompey is deliberately making a long story in order to avoid a direct answer. He does not want to say what it was that Froth did to Mistress Elbow, and so he makes all the objections and brings in all the irrelevancies he can think of. He even picks up Elbow's mistake of "respected" for "suspected" and uses it to create further confusion, but this is an act he is putting on. When Escalus turns to him and accuses him of being a bawd, he is shrewd and articulate enough in his own defense: "If your worship will take order for the drabs and the knaves, you need not to fear the bawds" (ll. 221–22).

There seems to be another verbal allusion to *Much Ado* in Elbow's reference to "a strange picklock," in III, ii, 15. Elbow is accusing Pompey to the Friar (Duke):

Friar. What offense hath this man made you, sir?
Elbow. Marry sir, he hath offended the law; and, sir, we take him to be a thief too, sir, for we have found upon him, sir, a strange picklock, which we have sent to the deputy.

One of the most hilarious blunders of the watch in *Much Ado* is that in which Borachio's "Seest thou not, I say, what a deformed thief this fashion is" (III, iii, 121) becomes to the First Watchman, "And one Deformed is one of them. I know him; 'a wears a lock" (that is, a lovelock, a wisp of hair worn beside the left ear). This is again transformed in Dogberry's report, "And also the watch heard them talk of one Deformed. They say he wears a key in his ear, and a lock hanging by it, and borrows money in God's name . . ." (V, i, 294–96). The "strange pick-lock" seems to be yet another twist to the same nonsense.

There are also echoes of *Much Ado* in such things as Angelo's impatient departure from the trial scene which parallels Leonato's impatient departure from Dogberry and Verges when they are trying to tell him of the villainy they have discovered. The Duke's crestfallen concern for his reputation after Lucio has slandered him so viciously to his face (while he is disguised as a Friar) is very like Benedick's when Beatrice takes advantage of his mask to slander him to his face.[22] In *Much Ado* Claudio is the name of the luckless lover, as it is in *Measure for Measure,* although the characters and situations of the two are antithetical. One proves overcautious, the other has been rash. Making "Claudio" the lover of "Juliet" has its ironic implications if, as Professor Leech suggests, "Shakespeare cannot have forgotten the earlier Juliet," [23] who also came to grief through a hasty and secret marriage.

There may be another reminiscence of *Romeo and Juliet* in the name "Escalus" given to the Duke's aged and trusted officer. "Escalus" is also the name of the Duke of Verona.

Perhaps, in the choice of names, allusion is intended, but elsewhere Shakespeare seems to have been careless about names, and some of the duplications may be due to coincidence, the result of a well-known tendency of authors to repeat themselves. Or perhaps the connection lay, not in the part, but in the actor. We do not know to what extent actors were "typed," but the association of the actor with a part in which he has been a notable success was probably as unavoidable then as now. We enjoy an actor's performance today partly by accepting the illusion he is creating, but also, and at the same time, partly by observing the way he is creating it. We marvel, for example, at the way Alfred Lunt acts with his whole body, especially with his torso, where others act chiefly with head and limbs. Moreover, we associate even the most versatile actors with character types. Many expressed shock at Sir Laurence Olivier's performance in *The Entertainer,* not specifically because they thought of him as Hamlet, or Henry V, but because the part seemed to do violence to his personality as it was known chiefly, or wholly, through his Shakespearean roles. We are simultaneously conscious of the actor as person and artist and of the character he is impersonating, of the reality and the illusion, and that dual consciousness enriches our pleasure. There is no reason to doubt that this was so in the audiences of Shakespeare's day, and probably to a greater degree, since the same plays were given over and over again, and the people who "haunted plays" must have seen the same play more than once, perhaps many times. The actors were well-known personalities, and not only the clowns, but the others also must have been able by a few words or a characteristic action to remind the audience of another part that actor had taken in another play. Such reminders are a kind of allusion, but we have probably lost the key to most of them.

A few can be traced with reasonable confidence. In *Much Ado,* Act IV, scene ii, the Quarto of 1600 reads "Kemp" and "Cowley" instead of "Dogberry" and "Verges" in the speech headings throughout the scene. Evidently Kemp created the part of Dogberry, or at least that part was intended for him; but he left the company about 1600 and was replaced by Robert Armin. Armin confessed that he had been "writ downe an Asse in his time," that is, he had played Dogberry.[24] It seems probable, therefore, that he also played Elbow, and perhaps that Cowley played Pompey. We might be tempted to go a step farther and to suggest that Cowley played Pistol in *The Merry Wives of Windsor*, which the Court had seen on November 4, and that he would play Pistol again in *Henry V* on January 7.

When Pompey goes off the stage, at the end of Act II, scene i, he utters an exit tag which is unlike anything else he says in this prose scene, or elsewhere, and which is much in the style of that other bawd, mine ancient Pistol. He says:

> Whip me! No, no, let carman whip his jade.
> The valiant heart's not whipt out of his trade.
> (II, i, 241–42)

In the *Merry Wives*, Pistol is dismissed by Falstaff and defies him, boasting:

> Tester I'll have in pouch when thou shalt lack,
> Base Phrygian Turk!   (I, iii, 96–97)

A little later, when Falstaff refuses to lend him money, he threatens:

> Why, then the world's mine oyster,
> Which I with sword will open.   (II, ii, 3–4)

Pompey is not otherwise like Pistol. It is as if the poet, writing the part of Pompey with the actor in mind who had played Pistol, gave him this exit tag to remind the audience (as he reminds the reader) of Pistol.

There seems also to be a suggestive echo of *Love's Labour's Lost* in the name "Pompey." Shakespeare revised *Love's Labour's Lost* in 1597,[25] and perhaps no further revision was made for the revival in 1604/5. In that play, the show of the Nine Worthies is produced, and Costard, the clown, plays the part of Pompey the Great. His is a leading part and he is taunted by the audience with his pretentious name (V, ii, 550–90, and again, 689–92).

In much the same way, when Pompey Bum is forced to confess to his name in Act II, scene i, the ground has been laid for Lucio's taunting of him with it in Act III, scene ii, ll. 41–80. He is simply "Clowne" in the speech headings throughout *Measure for Measure,* and he has at first been called in the text Mistress Overdone's "tapster." Shakespeare could hardly have forgotten Costard's enactment of Pompey the Great, and so we seem justified in regarding the name given to Mistress Overdone's bawd as preparation for a repetition of that bit of comedy. The King did not see *Love's Labour's Lost* at this time, and the Queen and the Court, who did see it, saw it *after Measure for Measure,* but the taunting scene would work as allusion either way. When Shakespeare was writing *Measure for Measure,* perhaps in the summer or autumn of 1604, while he probably knew which of his plays were to be used for the Christmas playing at court, he could hardly have known what the order of their presentation would be. It is even possible that the same clown who played Costard in the revival of *Love's Labour's Lost* in 1597 played Pompey in *Measure for Measure.* This was not Armin, since he had not yet joined the company. If Cowley was a good enough comedian to play end man to Kemp's Dogberry, he may very well have played Costard as well as Pompey Bum.

Speculation about the actors of the various parts is nebulous at best, but there seems to be enough evidence for this play to support the contention that one of Shakespeare's objectives in creating it was to recommend the members of his company, or rather enable them to recommend themselves, to their patron and monarch. I have already pointed out how first Isabella, then Angelo, then Claudio, and finally the Duke are given "big" scenes. Even Escalus and the Provost have their special moments.

As for reminiscences of others of Shakespeare's plays, Isabella's speech on mercy has reminded several critics of Portia's, and probably the same boy played both in 1604/5, but *The Merchant of Venice* was being saved for the end of the season. The court had not seen it when it saw *Measure for Measure,* and the two speeches have little in common except the theme, which could be counted on to meet with the King's approval (in theory) at any time.

Lucio has been called a Jonsonian humors character, but the King had not yet seen any of Jonson's comedies. Students seem sometimes overeager to claim that Jonson, or Fletcher, or some other younger dramatist influenced Shakespeare. Perhaps "stimulated" would be a better word. King James took considerable pride in his learning, which meant, of course, classical learning, and his approval would perhaps have had more influence than Jonson's in turning the drama toward classical models. There may be a concession to the classical unity of time in the repeated "tomorrows" which hurry the action of *Measure for Measure* along; and as for unity of place, everything happens in Vienna, and in Acts III and V everything happens in one place.

The stage is never emptied throughout the act. Act V is notable for the number of speakers on the scene at one time, and for the management of the dialogue so that more than three persons are involved in the same conversation. This kind of talk is more difficult to write and to direct than that which involves only two or three speakers. Shakespeare manages this complex talk so that it gives quickness and vitality to the whole scene, contributing to the suspense by keeping the audience alert. This effect of general conversation was seldom achieved either in classical times or in later ones.

There are echoes of one other earlier play which are clear enough. When, or where, the King saw *Hamlet* is not recorded, but it is hardly probable that he had not. At any rate, in addition to the echo of Polonius in the Duke's opening speech, several critics have seen a parallel between Hamlet's soliloquy on death, "To be or not to be," and Claudio's description of the terrors of death in his plea, "Sweet sister, let me live." But the most interesting parallel is that between Angelo's inability to pray and King Claudius's. The phrasing of the two speeches is entirely different. Claudius begins:

> O, my offence is rank, it smells to heaven;
> It hath the primal eldest curse upon't,
> A brother's murder. Pray can I not,
> Though inclination be as sharp as will.
> My stronger guilt defeats my strong intent, . . .
>
> (III, iii, 36–72)

Angelo is more specific and analytical:

> When I would pray and think, I think and pray
> To several [that is, different] subjects: heaven
>   hath my empty words,
> Whilst my invention, hearing not my tongue,
> Anchors on Isabel: heaven in my mouth,
> As if I did but only chew his name. . . .   (II, iv, 1–7)

In King Claudius' words we can see a troubled soul, but in Angelo's no more than a troubled mind. It is not that Shakespeare has lost, for the moment, the power to express strong emotion in simple and moving metaphor, but that he needs, in *Hamlet,* to arouse some audience-sympathy for Claudius, as well as to point up the irony of the situation: Hamlet's refusal to kill the King at prayer for fear his soul will go to heaven, while the King laments his inability to pray. Angelo's argument with himself is prelude to his lewd proposal to Isabella. At that point sympathy for Angelo would be out of place, and a comic echo of a striking scene in *Hamlet* would help to keep the mood light enough so that the audience could enjoy Angelo's subsequent embarrassment in trying to make Isabella understand his proposal.

Shakespeare is like a great organist whose instrument is his audience. He modulates their response with perfect skill by controlling the tone, the duration, and the tempo of each part with a sureness which even the most shallow and inept of directors and actors cannot entirely miss, however they distort, cut, transpose, and misinterpret. So here, King Claudius' struggle with his conscience, his desire and inability to make his peace with heaven give him a depth of tragic intensity which humanizes him, gives him a third dimension, and puts in him the warm breath of life, so lacking in *Sejanus*, for example. This is the first time we have seen him alone, and we discover in him an inner life which is different (as it is in all of us) from the personality he shows others. In *Measure for Measure* we have somewhat the same situation in a very different mood. Angelo is struggling with temptation, not failing in true repentance of a crime already committed; his temptation is not ambition but lust, a much less heroic passion, and Angelo's lines accordingly lack depth of emotion. Like Claudius's, his choice is expressed in terms of heaven and hell, but the words, the thoughts, and the figures of speech are almost flippant, as "Let's write 'good Angel' on the devil's horn" (that is, let's call bad, good). The effect is to keep the scene from developing tragic depth or emotion. The reminiscence of Claudius is playful parody, further lightened by Angelo's description of his emotions on hearing that Isabella has come to see him. His blood rushes to his heart, he is suffocated, like "a well-wished king" whose subjects "crowd to his presence." There

is an absurd disproportion in the comparison. We are being prepared not for tragic, but for comic, events.

One other striking parallel between *Measure for Measure* and
another play of Shakespeare's is the plot device of the bed-trick.
It is usually assumed that *All's Well That Ends Well* is the
earlier play, and that Shakespeare made use of the substitution-
in-bed again to save Isabella's chastity, but the development could
have been the other way. Having used the trick as a minor part of
the plot of *Measure for Measure,* he may have developed it into
a main plot in *All's Well.*[26] It is suggested that, because the
bed-trick is inherent in the plot material of *All's Well,* but is
added to that of *Measure for Measure,* therefore "we might assume that it would appear first in a source-story and be added to
another source only subsequently." [27] But can we suppose the
plays were not only written one at a time, but that the poet
labored at his source-stories one at a time, so that what he had
not yet used he did not yet know about? The absurdity of such an
assumption is apparent once we take it out and look at it. For
reasons which must be explained elsewhere, I believe that *Measure for Measure* was completed before, and not after, *All's
Well.*[28] Nothing in the double use of this plot motif precludes
that order of composition.

It seems safe to conclude that the King had seen *Hamlet,* and
that he had recently enjoyed *Much Ado,* especially the part of
Dogberry. Such names as "Juliet," "Pompey," and "Claudio" may
allude to other plays, *Romeo and Juliet, Love's Labour's Lost,
Much Ado,* in which characters bore these names; or the names
may have been suggested to Shakespeare's mind by the actors for
whom he was writing the parts: that is, the actor who played
Claudio in *Much Ado* might have suggested "Claudio" as the
name of the part being written for him in *Measure for Measure.*

In so stable and long lasting a company as Shakespeare belonged to (they had been together for ten years), it would be strange if he did not anticipate the casting even while he was creating the play.[29] In *Measure for Measure,* he gave his fellows lines which would invite recollection of other parts they had played, as well as of other plays he had written.

These echoes, as allusions for the amusement of King James, perhaps add a little to our knowledge of the stage history of a few plays, but their chief importance lies in what they show us about the nature of the royal performance of *Measure for Measure* on December 26, 1604.

Probably there were other echoes of past performances, now no longer identifiable. One very short scene in Act IV which has never been explained may be a friendly and humorous gesture to include other playwrights who were either friends of the poet or contributors to their repertory. The Duke is arranging for his return, and for the play-acting which is to bring Angelo to repentance. He sends messages to his most trusted friends and supporters:

> Go call at Flavius' house,
> And tell him where I stay; give the like notice
> To Valencius, Rowland, and to Crassus,
> And bid them bring the trumpets to the gate,
> But send me Flavius first.   (IV, v, 6–10)

Then Varrius enters and is named twice in the Duke's greeting, as if his name was important:

> I thank thee, Varrius; thou hast made good haste.
> Come, we will walk; there's other of our friends
> Will greet us here anon, my gentle Varrius.   *Exeunt.*

We suspect topical matter because *Rowland* stands out as not a Latin name, and as the well-known pen name of Michael Drayton. The others are all names of Roman *gens,* and may allude to Ben Jonson's use of Latin names for the characters in his first two comedies, or they may allude to other playwrights. *Valencius* may be from Valentini, the Roman name for the inhabitants of the southern part of Scotland, or it may be intended to suggest a playwright with a beard. Some of the names Shakespeare had used elsewhere. Flavius is the name of one of the tribunes in the first scene of *Julius Caesar,* and Varrius is the name of a friend of Pompey's in *Antony and Cleopatra* (which was not yet written). Lucius Crassus was an orator and triumvir contemporary with Cicero. The Duke may be sending for other playwrights, since he is about to produce a play, or possibly for actors. The names seem to be a bit of mystification for the contemporary audience, which they could solve, but we cannot.

In general, there is little reason to question that this play was conceived, among other things, as a show piece, a special vehicle for exhibition of the skill of both the playwright and the actors. The climactic succession of "big scenes," for Isabella, Angelo, Claudio, and finally the Duke, is brilliantly contrived. And what of the Duke? We can be sure that he could not, in the wildest imaginings, be mistaken for King James, but how was that dissociation made absolutely sure?

VIII · The Duke as Actor and Playwright

Preoccupation with the charms and problems of Isabella has obscured the fact that the Duke is as much the hero and leading character of this play as Prospero is of *The Tempest*. He sets it in motion by abdicating and endowing the untried Angelo with absolute power. As the struggle between Isabella and Angelo develops in the second act he simply stands by (in disguise); but when, in the third act, that struggle reaches an impasse, he steps forward and takes over. Theirs is not the primary, but the secondary, struggle of the play; it is the subplot, not the main plot. Isabella submits to the Duke's direction, and he takes on the responsibility of saving both Isabella and Claudio. He also, at the end of Act III, undertakes to bring Angelo to justice. In Act IV he is chiefly active in outwitting Angelo and saving Claudio; and in Act V he brings about a just and merciful end of all conflicts: Isabella's with Angelo, Mariana's with Angelo, Angelo's with his conscience, and his own with both Angelo and Isabella.

Isabella's struggle for her brother's life, her struggle with Angelo, cannot be the main conflict of the play because by the end of Act III *both* Angelo and Isabella have failed, Angelo in the administration of justice and the seduction of Isabella, and

Isabella in the practice of mercy. The Duke is left to straighten out the mess they have made, and to teach them to do better.

The major struggle of the play is that of the Duke with Angelo. The play begins with it and ends when it is resolved by Angelo's sincere repentance which predicates reform, and by the Duke's resumption of his responsibilities as ruler. In the larger implications of *Measure for Measure,* Angelo and Isabella play the part of mankind, not in the simple story of Adam and Eve, but in the universal frame of every man's fall through his pride (that is, over-confidence in himself), his appetites, and his inexperience; and the Duke embodies the Divine mercy which watches over man, giving him power to do both good and evil, yet guiding, teaching, and, when he is truly and humbly repentant, forgiving and saving from the worser consequences of his folly. King James wrote that the King is a God on earth, and as he is responsible for the administration of justice, so is a Duke, or any governor, in his smaller world. The Duke as Divine Providence is therefore in keeping with the King's exalted concept of the duty of a ruler.

The Duke's is a great part, and a difficult one to act. The action is kept firmly on the human level. He is no Prospero, no wizard. He is neither omnipotent nor omniscient, since he is sometimes mistaken; and he saves the situation by his cleverness, not by his power. On the other hand, the whole play, and especially the last act, provides the actor of this part with magnificent opportunity for a display of his skill. Act V opens with the Duke's pretense that he has been away, knows nothing of what has been going on, and has complete confidence in Angelo. He is pretending, or play-acting still. Having for three acts played the Friar, he now plays the returning Duke in an elaborate five-act play-within-a-play.

This playlet, which he has planned, begins as Isabella enters and kneels to beg for "justice," and make her wild accusations, as she has been instructed. In ordering her arrest, the Duke asks the leading question: "Who knew of your intent and coming hither?" She names "Friar Lodowick" (that is, the Duke in disguise), and Lucio speaks up to accuse the Friar of speaking against the Duke. Friar Peter, in Friar Lodowick's defense, accuses Isabella of having lied (as she has, having been instructed to do so by him!). As Isabella is led away in custody, Mariana is brought in veiled.

This is the end of Act I and the beginning of Act II of the Duke's play. The interval is marked by six lines (163–68) of comment by the Duke. In Act II Mariana refuses to show her face "until my husband bid me," and after some mystification created by the Duke's blind questions ("What, are you married?" etc.), and interruptions by Lucio, she unmasks and makes her accusations against Angelo. The Duke pretends to think that she also is lying. Angelo asks scope "to find this practice out," and so the Duke, still playing his part of having been away, appoints Angelo and Escalus to examine the two women. Meanwhile the Provost (who, the audience has been told, "knows our purpose and our plot" [IV, v, 2]) is sent to bring Friar Lodowick. The Duke must, of course, himself be absent when the Friar reappears, and so he excuses himself and exits, bringing Act II of the Duke's play to an end. The interval between Acts II and III is filled by Escalus' questioning of Lucio about the Friar (ll. 259–76).

In Act III the Duke reenters (disguised as Friar Lodowick) along with the Provost and Isabella. Escalus undertakes to question the Friar, being guided only by what he has heard of him from Lucio, and when the Friar criticizes the Duke for his "unjust" behavior in turning the women over for questioning to the man they have accused, Escalus hotly defends the Duke. It is a wonderfully ridiculous scene, in which Escalus acts in perfect good faith, within the limits of his ignorance, and ends by ordering the Friar (Duke) "to the rack." The Friar double-talks his way through this scene, as when he replies:

> Be not so hot. The Duke
> Dare no more stretch this finger of mine than he
> Dare rack his own: his subject am I not,
> Nor here provincial.   (ll. 311–14)

This is all true, but those who know the Friar as the Duke are amused at the way this truth deceives those who do not know. Elsewhere he is more cryptic, as when Escalus exclaims:

> How! know you where you are?
> *Duke.* Respect to your great place; and let the devil
>   Be sometime honored for his burning throne.
>   [That is, "Give the devil his due."]
>   Where is the Duke? 'Tis he should hear me speak. (ll. 289–92)

His denunciation of himself is often quoted as a true picture of the Vienna of the play, but he is actually intent on deliberately provoking Escalus into ordering his arrest. He says:

> My business in this state
> Made me a looker-on here in Vienna,
> Where I have seen corruption boil and bubble
> Till it o'errun the stew. Laws for all faults,
> But faults so countenanced that the strong statutes
> Stand like the forfeits in a barber's shop,
> As much in mock as mark.   (ll. 314–20)

This is simply a restatement of what the Duke said in I, iii, 19–31, to Friar Thomas, to explain his conduct in pretending to go abroad and deputizing Escalus and Angelo to rule in his place. He is stigmatizing his own failure in government, and the general corruption of the world. Escalus orders the Friar to prison, and Angelo asks Lucio for further charges against him. Lucio obliges by accusing the Friar of saying outrageous things about the Duke which, the audience knows, Lucio himself has said.

The interplay of true and false, of what has happened and what is pretended, reaches a climax when poor, uninformed Escalus orders the Provost to lead the Friar to prison. The Provost, still acting the part assigned to him by the Duke, makes an ineffectual gesture of arresting him, and Angelo orders Lucio to assist. So it is Lucio who pulls off the Friar's hood and becomes "the first knave that e'er mad'st a duke."

This is, of course, the turning point of the playlet. The Duke drops his pretense of having been away and rounds on Angelo:

> Hast thou or word, or wit, or impudence
> That yet can do thee office?

Angelo immediately recognizes that the Duke knows all, and begs for "immediate sentence" of death; but instead he is sent out to be married to Mariana. Act III ends with their exit, and Act IV begins with their reentry as man and wife. The short interval, or interact, is filled by Isabella's apology to the Duke (ll. 376–94) for having

> employed and pained
Your unknown sovereignty,

and the Duke's apology for "your brother's death," a fiction which must be maintained until he has tested her charity and completed his disciplining of Angelo. With the reentry of Angelo and Mariana (Act IV), the Duke invites Isabella to demand "an Angelo for Claudio, death for death." This brings Mariana to plead for Angelo's life, and, when the Duke proves firm, to beg Isabella to kneel beside her (and so achieve true charity). Even after Isabella has made her plea, the Duke thinks of "another fault"—Claudio was beheaded at an unusual hour (which was illegal in England). He reprimands the Provost for it and relieves him of his office. The Provost, still playing his assigned role, now confesses that he has failed to execute Barnardine, and is sent to fetch him.

This exit marks the end of Act IV, and the interval is filled by Escalus' expression of regret that Angelo "should slip so grossly" and Angelo's reply that he craves "death more willingly than mercy" (ll. 466–73). Then the Provost returns with Barnardine and a muffled figure who turns out to be Claudio. The Duke, obviously with his tongue in his cheek, says of Barnardine, "There was a friar told me of this man," and he pardons Barnardine for all his "earthly faults." Then he asks the Provost, "What muffled fellow's that?" and the last pretense of the playlet is ended. Isabella is reunited with her brother; Angelo "perceives he's safe," since Claudio is not dead. The Duke, failing to get Isabella's attention to his proposal of marriage, turns to Lucio with "here's one in place I cannot pardon." He sentences him, for slandering the Duke, to be married to the woman he has wronged, then whipped, and finally hanged; but he immediately remits all but the marriage, and so Act V of the playlet ends.

In the last fifteen lines the Duke sums up his judgments: Claudio is to marry Julietta, Angelo is to love Mariana, Escalus is promised a reward, and the Provost "a worthier place." He remembers to order Angelo to forgive the Provost for substituting the head of Ragozine for Claudio's, and finally, he makes a formal proposal to Isabella and clears the stage:

> So bring us to our palace, where we'll show
> What's yet behind, that's meet you all should know.

The last act makes a brilliant ending to a witty comedy, providing an amazing exhibition of the actor's art for the part of the Duke. The regular, five-act structure of the play-within-a-play is too complete and clear to be accidental, marked off as it is by exits and entrances and provided in every case with a few lines of dialogue which, choruslike, fill the interact so that the stage need never be cleared, since this is also Act V of the play. Each act of the playlet follows the usual pattern. The first presents the situation and begins the action; Act II provides complication; Act III covers the point-of-no-return; Act IV provides the counteraction completing the conflict; Act V supplies the denouement and the new norm:

Act I. Isabella accuses Angelo according to her instructions. Her accusation is doubted, and she is arrested (ll. 19–162).

Act II. Mariana accuses Angelo of the same crime. The two women are turned over to Angelo and Escalus for trial (ll. 167–258).

Act III. Friar Lodowick is brought in, accused of libel of the Duke, and revealed as the Duke in disguise. He sentences Angelo to marry Mariana (ll. 277–375).

Act IV. Angelo is sentenced to death for executing Claudio. Mariana pleads for him, and Isabella, by adding her plea to Mariana's, demonstrates her charity. Barnardine is sent for (ll. 395–465).

Act V. Barnardine is forgiven his crimes. Claudio is reunited with Isabella (and Julietta). Angelo is pardoned. Lucio is suitably punished, and the Duke proposes to Isabella (ll. 474–519).

Just as the main plot builds up to a sharply marked turning point when the Duke, disguised as a Friar, takes command of a chaotic situation, so in this play-within-a-play the turning point comes when the Friar is unmasked, proves to be the Duke, and immediately takes control. Even the language of the two scenes is repeated in reverse, for, whereas in Act III of the main plot the lines suddenly drop into prose as the Friar comes forward to help Isabella, so in the playlet a scene which has deteriorated into prose as Lucio slanders the Friar and Escalus orders the Friar to prison (V, 322–51) turns sharply into blank verse in the first speech of the Duke after his disguise has been pulled off, and remains on the higher level of diction and rhythm for the remainder of the play.

Act V of *Measure for Measure* is a complete five-act play in miniature, directed by the Duke, its author, except, apparently, for one element in it, the repeated interruptions and impertinences of Lucio. The disruptive activities of this minor character are amazing and puzzling. Quiller-Couch complains: "We find it hard to take the final scene seriously, what with the insufferable Lucio ambling up and down to turn the whole affair into 'comedy' in spite of itself, and the Duke abetting by lending him so much attention distraught from the true and weightier justice in hand, when a word might dismiss the fribble to the stocks." [1]

Lucio's interruptions begin when he breaks in to support Isabella (ll. 74–85). Next he slanders Friar Lodowick to the Duke (ll. 127–36, 149). Again, in the second "act" of the playlet, he speaks up (ll. 179–90) and the Duke silences him with difficulty. He breaks in on the Duke's questioning of Mariana and Angelo (ll. 212–13), and answers Escalus' inquiry about the character of the Friar with more abuse (ll. 261–85) until Escalus commands him to be silent. He gets in a word again in Act III (l. 302), and is rude and abusive to the Friar (ll. 324–37), ending with name-calling as he pulls off the Friar's hood (ll. 348–51). The discovery of the Duke under the Friar's hood has a quieting effect on him, however. After his comment, "This may prove worse than hanging" (l. 356), he is silent for over two hundred lines, until the Duke turns to him with the remark:

> And yet here's one in place I cannot pardon.
> You, sirrah, that knew me for a fool, a coward,
> One all of luxury, an ass, a madman,
> Wherein have I so deserved of you,
> That you extol me thus? (ll. 495–99)

Lucio is still irrepressible: " 'Faith, my lord, I spoke it but according to the trick. If you will hang me for it, you may; but I had rather it would please you, I might be whipped." The Duke accepts the suggestion: "Whipped first, sir, and hanged after." But if any woman will complain that he has wronged her, Lucio is to be married and then whipped and hanged. The Duke has finally found Lucio's weak spot, and reduced him to humility:

Lucio. I beseech your highness, do not marry me to a whore. Your highness said even now, I made you a duke; good my lord, do not recompense me in making me a cuckold.
Duke. Upon mine honor, thou shalt marry her.
Thy slanders I forgive, and therewithal
Remit thy other forfeits.

He seems not really to forgive the slanders, however, for when Lucio protests once more, "Marrying a punk, my lord, is pressing to death, whipping, and hanging," the Duke responds, "Slandering a prince deserves it." The words are addressed more to King James than to the fictions of the play.

This is the last we see of Lucio. It is also the end of the play. His impertinence has been carried very far, so far that we might ask, has Shakespeare for once overworked a comic device? His persistent slandering, the dramatic purpose of which E. K. Chambers found "not quite clear"[2] becomes clear enough when we view the play as created to amuse the writer and the readers of the *Basilikon Doron*. His activities in scandalmongering do not account, however, for his activities in Act V of interrupting the serious business of the little playlet, and annoying the Duke repeatedly. These interruptions have the dramatic value of creating tension and, as Quiller-Couch observed, of keeping the scene comic. The main action stops while the Duke wrestles with the business of silencing him, and each time he speaks the Duke's mounting irritation threatens to erupt. Yet Lucio's punishment is saved for the very end of the play, providing a comic echo and anticlimax for Angelo's. Angelo had given as his main reason for not marrying Mariana that "her reputation was disvalued/In levity" (V, 219–20). He suspects her honesty; Lucio more than suspects Kate Keepdown's, and so provides a comic parallel.

Lucio's interruptions seem to try the patience of the Duke. It is true that his charges against the Friar are dramatically necessary to force the revelation that the Friar is the Duke in disguise, but Lucio's fate could have been settled in the first moment of his disclosure of the Duke under the Friar's hood. Why is it saved to the very end of the play? Quiller-Couch says, "It is one of the puzzles of the play that the jackanapes Lucio should take so much of the limelight as he does in the *finale,* and the Duke waste so much attention upon him, while Isabella and Claudio

—the two that most count—stand silent in the background." [3]

This is the Duke's playlet. We have seen him busily planning it and instructing the actors of it; and, when he comes on the scene, in Act V, to take the leading role, he is in perfect control of the situation. Everything goes exactly as planned—except for the interruptions of Lucio. These seem irrelevant, and yet they bring about the dramatic disclosure which is central to the Duke's play. He could not have managed without Lucio. Even when he seems to be a disrupting and impertinent distraction, Lucio is serving the Duke's purpose, like all the others. The play-within-a-play has suggested puppetry to several commentators, and Lucio, too, is the Duke's puppet, serving his turn even when he seems to be most irritating. He is like Charlie McCarthy talking back to Edgar Bergen.

However, the humor of that situation requires that the audience should understand clearly, and immediately, the relation between the puppet and the puppeteer. The Duke as a character in *Measure for Measure* does not suggest the puppeteering relationship to Lucio strongly enough to make Lucio's apparent insubordination funny. The Duke's authorship of the playlet, while it is prepared for in Act IV, is not fully patent until the play is almost over. In the early scenes of Act V the audience is puzzled by the Duke's pretense that he has been away and knows nothing of what has gone on in his absence. In other words, the actor in his persona as Duke is busy playing the unknowing Duke. It is only in his persona as author that he is the puppeteer.

If we could imagine that Shakespeare himself acted the part of the Duke, then the Duke's irritation at Lucio's impertinences becomes hilarious in the familiar pattern of Edgar Bergen's annoyance at Charlie McCarthy. Indeed, such a supposition illuminates several dark places in the play, and especially in the behavior of the Duke. For example, when the Friar comes bustling into the prison, confidently expecting Claudio's reprieve, an order arrives for his immediate execution, and the Duke-Friar is hard put to it to save Claudio. But if the actor of the part is also the author of the play, there is a good deal of humor in the situation. And when the Provost suggests substituting the head of Ragozine, who "died this morning," and the Friar-Duke piously exclaims, "O, 'tis an accident that heaven provides" (IV, iii, 66–74), with what delight the audience would recognize that the author-actor himself had provided it! The complex of awareness available to the audience would be tedious to analyze in any detail.[4] For example, in this scene, if Shakespeare himself played the part of the Duke, then he was playing three roles at once, that of author-creator of the situation, that of actor-Duke-manager of the whole play, and that of the disguised character, Friar Lodowick in this scene, as in most of Acts II, III, and IV. In Act V he would be playing himself as the author of the Duke, and the Duke who is author of the playlet, and who is pretending to be the returning Duke. He also returns to the part of Friar Lodowick in this act, so that Lucio, whom, as author, he has created, can pull off his Friar's hood. Moreover, as author, he has created not only the interruptions, but also Lucio's scandals about the Duke at which he, as Duke, is so incensed. If, as I have argued, Shakespeare wrote the play for the Christmas revels, for the purpose of amusing King James, and of recommending to him his company of actors and himself as their chief playwright, it would surely be appropriate that he should write a leading part for himself, and one which not only showed him to advantage as actor, but, in the last act, showed this actor as planning, producing, and acting in a play.

The hypothesis that Shakespeare played the part of the Duke explains one further puzzle in this play. We can be sure that, in a play so patently written to please and amuse King James, Shakespeare would be careful to avoid any suggestion that the Duke *represents* the King. Yet he makes the Duke voice the King's principles of government as set forth in the *Basilikon Doron,* and attempt to put them into practice; he goes even further and has the Duke express a personal idiosyncrasy of the King's, his dislike of crowds and "Aves vehement." There is delicious irony in having Shakespeare, the actor, express such a distaste for applause! But, more important, if the author himself acted the part of the Duke, then there could be no suggestion that the Duke was, or represented, King James. He *is* Shakespeare, acting a play which exemplifies what King James had written about kingcraft (that is, he is the King's puppet), and, in the last act, producing a play he has created (as the Duke) to resolve all difficulties and make everything come out right in the end. Shakespeare as actor and playwright is the "God on earth" of his play, manipulating the other characters like puppets, and creating Lucio, the puppet who talks back to his creator. He is the God-Ruler in his world of make-believe, as King James thought himself to be in the real world.

IX · Shakespeare as Actor

One of the great losses which sluttish time has cost us is the record of Shakespeare's acting, and especially of the parts which he wrote for himself. Instead of this important information, we have two eighteenth-century legends, one that he played Adam in *As You Like It,* and the other, that he played the Ghost in *Hamlet.* His first biographer, Nicholas Rowe, writing in 1709, said that he was "not an extraordinary actor," and called the part of the Ghost in *Hamlet* "the top of his performance."[1] Rowe claimed to have most of his information from Betterton who, according to John Downes, was instructed in the part of Hamlet by Davenant, who had seen Mr. Taylor act it. Taylor claimed to have known Shakespeare, although he did not join the King's Men until 1619, after Shakespeare's death. At best, therefore, the story that Shakespeare played the Ghost in *Hamlet* is fourth-hand hearsay.

In Rowe's time, four or five generations after Shakespeare's death, when Dryden was already dead, and Pope was beginning his meteoric career, Shakespeare was deprecated as an untutored genius who wrote formless plays that must be (and were) re-written and "corrected" for the more refined and elegant stage of

Queen Anne's day. Obviously, a natural genius so ignorant of the art of playwriting, could not have been much of an actor!

Ironically enough, the notion that Shakespeare was an untutored genius who "wanted Arte" [2] was largely created by Shakespeare's defenders. Ben Jonson, in the glowing tribute printed in the First Folio, started the controversy by saying:

> Nature her selfe was proud of his designes,
> And ioy'd to weare the dressing of his lines!

Yet he does not deny that Shakespeare also possessed art.

> Yet must I not giue Nature all: Thy Art,
> My gentle *Shakespeare,* must enjoy a part.
> For though the *Poets* matter, Nature be,
> His Art doth giue the fashion. And, that he,
> Who casts to write a living line, must sweat,
> (Such as thine are) and strike the second heat
> Vpon the *Muses* anuile: . . . . .
> For a good *Poet's* made, as well as borne,
> And such wert thou.[3]

Jonson's assertion that Shakespeare *worked* at writing aroused the indignation of Shakespeare's young admirer, Leonard Digges, stepson of his friend William Russell, who retorted in a poem which was not published until 1640, although it was obviously written for the first folio.[4] It begins:

> Poets are borne not made, when I would prove
> This truth, the glad remembrance I must love
> Of never dying *Shakespeare,* who alone,
> Is argument enough to make that one.
> First that he was a Poet none would doubt,
> That heard th'applause of what he sees set out
> Imprinted; where thou hast (I will not say)

Reader his Workes (for to contrive a Play
To him twas none) the patterne of all wit,
Art without art unparaleld as yet.
Next Nature onely helpt him, for look thorow
This whole Booke, thou shalt find he doth not borrow,
One phrase from Greekes, nor Latines imitate,
Nor once from vulgar Languages Translate,
Nor Plagiari-like from others gleane,
Nor begges he from each witty friend a Scene
To peece his Acts with . . . .[5]

Jonson's advocacy of art, to be learned by imitation of the ancients, is clearly Digges's target. Jonson's famous stricture, "hee
never blotted out line . . . would he had blotted a thousand," [6]
is perhaps a comment on the words in Heminges' and Condell's
address to the readers of the First Folio, "as he was a happie imi-
tator of Nature, was a most gentle expresser of it. His mind and
hand went together: And what he thought, he vttered with that
easinesse, that wee haue scarce receiued from him a blot in his
papers." [7]

The controversy was older than the first folio (1623), for
Francis Beaumont declared himself on the side of Shakespeare
against Jonson's "art," in a poem addressed "To M^r· B: J:"

And from all Learninge keep these lines as cleere
As Shakespeares best are, which our heires shall heare
Preachers apte to their auditors to showe
how farr sometimes a mortall man may goe
by the dimme light of Nature . . . .[8]

Some of what follows is cryptic, but his defence of Shakespeare
as a natural genius, against Jonson's "art," the imitation of the
ancients, belongs to the background against which we must see

Milton's tribute in 1630, "toth' shame of slow-endeavouring art,/ Thy easie numbers flow," [9] and his familiar lines in "L'Allegro":

> Then to the well-trod stage anon,
> If *Jonson's* learned Sock be on,
> Or sweetest *Shakespeare,* fancy's child,
> Warble his native Wood-notes wild.   (ll. 131–34)[10]

Thomas Fuller also took sides in the controversy, saying, "*Poeta non fit, sed nescitur,* one is not *made,* but *born* a Poet. Indeed his Learning was very little," and he goes on to contrast Jonson's learning with Shakespeare's wit and invention.[11] About the time of the Restoration, John Ward, Vicar of Stratford, recorded in his notebook, "I have heard y[t] Mr Shakespeare was a natural wit, without any art at all." [12] So an artistic controversy has degenerated into a cliché of the ignorant. Shakespeare had no art at all, therefore how could he have been expert in the art of the actor?

Something of the old wives' tales current about the poet in Rowe's time may be gathered from the report of Rowe's contemporary and rival, Charles Gildon, who wrote, "I have been told that he writ the scene of the Ghost in *Hamlet,* at his House which bordered the Charnel-House and Church-yard." [13] The early eighteenth century is the period of darkest ignorance about the Elizabethan stage in general and about Shakespeare and his plays in particular. Four generations after Shakespeare's death, no one any longer remembered him or his times, and no one had begun the search for written records. Even the parish register at Stratford seems to have been unknown to Rowe, who thought that he had three daughters, and that Judith was the eldest.

E. K. Chambers says mildly that the story that Shakespeare acted the part of Adam in *As You Like It* is "dubious in its details." [14] It was not recorded until the mid-eighteenth century, and then it was represented as coming from a "brother" of Shakespeare's who lived until after the Restoration! Shakespeare's brothers all died before 1616. Chambers further says that Shakespeare's name "drops out of the actor-lists after *Every Man in His Humour* (1598) and *Sejanus* (1603)." [15] For "the actor-lists" we must understand "the lists of actors *in Jonson's plays*," for those are the only lists we have.[16] All that we can properly deduce, therefore, is that after the failure of *Sejanus*,[17] Shakespeare acted no more in Jonson's plays, that is, he did not act in *Volpone* (1605), *The Alchemist* (1610), nor in *Cataline* (1611). This is understandable if, as tradition has it, Jonson blamed Shakespeare for the failure of *Sejanus*.[18] The note after the text of *Volpone* names only six actors, four of whom were among the six "principall Comoedians" who acted in *Every Man Out of His Humour*. Shakespeare did not act in that play, either, although it was performed in 1599, several years before the *Sejanus* failure. In a stock company, such as theirs was, not every leading actor takes a principal part in every play.

Chambers speculates that Shakespeare gave up acting, but he does not suggest when. He says, "It may be that after a time his plays, together, perhaps, with the oversight of their production, were accepted as sufficient return for his share in the company. If so, he presumably did not get any special payment for them." [19] This is pure speculation. There is no reason to question that Shakespeare acted at court in the production of *Every Man in His Humour* during the Christmas season of 1604/5, as he had in the original production of 1598. His name heads the list of actors in this play, which Jonson caused to be printed in his *Workes* (1616). He is named as one of the principal actors in *Sejanus* in 1603, or, more probably, in 1604.

In contrast to the gossip picked up by Rowe, almost a century after Shakespeare's death, are contemporary statements that he was an excellent actor, and that he "plaid some Kingly parts." Scholars have ignored, or discounted, this evidence, probably for the same reason that his contemporaries seldom mention his acting. After the publication of *Venus and Adonis* and *Lucrece*, early in his career, tributes were paid to him as a poet, not because his poetry was better than his acting, but because the poet's calling was so much more honorable than the actor's.

Robert Greene's famous diatribe (1592) was aimed at the actors, "those Puppets (I meane) that spake from our mouths, . . . there is an vpstart Crow, beautified with our feathers, that with his *Tygers hart wrapt in a Players hyde,* supposes he is as well able to bombast out a blanke verse as the best of you . . . those buckram Gentlemen . . . these painted monsters . . ." [20] Henry Chettle, in his apology, says "my selfe have seene his demeanor no lesse ciuill than he excelent in the qualitie he professes," that is, the quality (or calling) of actor.[21] This statement has been discounted as a peacemaking gesture, yet it seems unquestionable that Shakespeare began his career as an actor before he began writing plays, and that he made his mark first as an actor. If he had been capable of no more than the minor parts Rowe's and Oldys' gossip assigned to him, he would hardly have made his way into an important place in the best acting company of his day, nor would he have continued to act for at least a decade after he had established himself as a productive and successful playwright, as Jonson's lists testify that he did.

There is other testimony to his ability as an actor. John Aubrey (1626–97), who was born fifty years nearer Shakespeare's time than was Rowe (b. 1674), reports that he "did act exceedingly well." [22] Aubrey also was reporting hearsay, but, unlike Rowe, he was untouched by eighteenth-century classical theory. He grew up in the time of Charles I, when Shakespeare's plays were still acted. He was an avid collector of gossip from his elders. He knew, for example, Sir Kenelm Digby, who had been a friend and patron of Ben Jonson. He knew Sir William Davenant, who was born ten years before Shakespeare died and who was an enthusiastic admirer of the poet, going so far as to claim that he was Shakespeare's bastard son.

A much better witness than Aubrey was John Davies of Hereford, a contemporary and personal friend of Shakespeare and Burbage, who testifies that Shakespeare "plaid some Kingly parts," and couples him with Burbage as "Stage plaiers" whom fortune "Guerdond not, to their desarts." [23] In his *Scourge of Folly* (1611) Davies published an epigram, "To our English Terence, Mr. Will. Shake-speare," in which he says,

> Some say (good *Will*) which I, in sport, do sing,
> Had'st thou not plaid some Kingly parts in sport,
> Thou had'st bin a companion for a *King;*
> And, beene a King among the meaner sort.[24]

The allusion is somewhat ambiguous, but it seems to mean that, if Shakespeare had not been a player, albeit of "Kingly parts," he might have been a companion of a king and ruled over lesser men (might, perhaps, have aspired to be Master of the Revels, as John Lyly did?). Just why playing kingly parts disqualified Shakespeare from being "a companion for a king" is easily explained. King James warned his son not to make "your sporters your counsellers," especially "Comedians and Balladines, for the Tyrants delighted most in them. . . ." [25] Perhaps Davies is alluding to this principle of the King's.

The best evidence of Shakespeare's preeminence as an actor is the coupling of his name with Burbage's in what actor-lists we have. The positions of the other names on such lists, and the Elizabethan concern for "precedence," insures that the order of names is not accidental. For *Every Man in His Humour* the names of the actors are arranged in two columns, with Shakespeare's at the head of the first, and Burbage's at the head of the second column. In *Sejanus* Burbage's name heads the first, and Shakespeare's the second column. Burbage would surely have played the part of Sejanus. In the license issued to the King's Men, May 19, 1603, Lawrence Fletcher heads the list, but Shakespeare's name is second and Burbage's third. Fletcher was not a member of the Chamberlain's Company (which was taken over *in toto* as the King's), but he had won the King's patronage by taking a troup to Scotland before 1603, and so he seems to have been included in the patent if not in the company.[26] The list for the issue of red cloth for the coronation procession names the actors in a different order. Shakespeare is first, then Augustine Phillipps, Lawrence Fletcher, John Hemminges, and fifth, Richard Burbage. Augustine Phillipps singles out Shakespeare as the first to be named in his will, calling him "my Fellowe William Shakespeare." [27] The "Fellowe" may, of course, mean "Fellow-sharer," but there is no evidence that anyone was a sharer in the company who was not an actor. The same epithet is applied to Henry Condell, Lawrence Fletcher, Robert Armin, Richard Cowley, Alexander Cook, and Nicholas Tooley. Christopher Beeston is described as "my Servaunte," and Samuell Gilborne as "my late apprentice." Nor does it seem probable that, if Shakespeare had given up acting and limited himself to writing plays, as Chambers suggests,[28] Phillipps would have named him among the actors. He first bequeaths five pounds to be shared among the hired men of the company, and then proceeds to the remembrance of named individuals, beginning with Shakespeare. Phillipps made his will on May 4, 1605. Jonson's list of the actors in *Sejanus* cannot refer to a time earlier than 1603, and in all probability refers to the summer or autumn of 1604. Shakespeare was still very much one of Augustine Phillipps' "fellows" in the spring of 1605—and not as a poor player of bit parts! To that status he was reduced by the ignorance and preconceptions of the early eighteenth century, which recognized no other art than neo-classical and assumed that he could not act because he could not write plays (to their taste). But since Rowe's gossip was accepted as truth, and since it is inconceivable that Shakespeare should have continued to act minor roles while writing what are now recognized as incomparable comedies and the greatest tragedies, human dignity required that he should stop acting. There is probably an element of snobbery here too, a feeling that so great a poet and playwright could not have stooped to the business of acting. But the truth is that, however his fellow poets valued him as a poet, his fellow actors regarded him as an actor comparable to Richard Burbage. When they gathered together his plays for the First Folio, they provided the volume with a list of "The Names of the Principall Actors in all these Playes," and they put his name at the head of the list. Then come Burbage, Heminges, etc. If Shakespeare had been a minor actor who turned playwright and gave up acting when he achieved fame in his more dignified profession, surely his fellow actors would not have put his name at the head of this list of "Principall Actors" above even Burbage. His authorship of the plays they were publishing was incomparably the greater dignity.

Significant of his position also is the fact that his name is frequently coupled with Burbage's. In addition to the epigram already quoted, John Davies twice mentions him along with

Burbage in tributes to actors. In his *Microcosmos* (1603), he writes:

> *Players,* I loue yee, and your *Qualitie,*
> As ye are Men, that pass time not abus'd:
> And some I love for *painting, poesie,*   [in the margin,
> And say fell *Fortune* cannot be excus'd,   "W.S. R.B."]
> That hath for better *uses* you refus'd:
> *Wit, Courage, good shape, good partes,* and all *good,*
> As long as al these *goods* are no *worse* vs'd,
> And though the *stage* doth staine pure gentle *bloud,*
> Yet generous yee are in *minde* and *moode.*[29]

The statement of the last couplet makes clear why the fame of Shakespeare's poetry so thoroughly eclipsed that of his acting. Again, in *The Civile Warres of Death and Fortune* (1605) Davies says of Fortune:

> Some followed her by acting all mens parts,
>   [in the margin, "Stage plaiers"]
> These on a Stage she rais'd (in scorne) to fall:
> And made them Mirrors, by their acting Arts,
> Wherein men saw their faults, thogh ne'r so small:
> Yet some she guerdond not, to their desarts;
>   [in the margin, "W.S. R.B."]
> But, othersome, were but ill-Action all. . . .[30]

Even the little joke recorded by John Manningham in his diary in 1602, "that William the Conquerour was before Rich. the 3.," while there is no need to regard it as true (we all know that such stories are invented and circulate today), shows how Shakespeare and Burbage were associated in the minds of their contemporaries as fellow *actors.*[31]

But the chief evidence that Shakespeare was "excellent in the quality" of actor is contained in the plays themselves, in the actability of every part he wrote, in the way he writes from inside a character, so that we can only say, "How true to life," "How right," "How typical." This quality of sympathetic understanding of a part, of imagining himself to be the character he is acting is necessary to the great actor, but what an asset it is also to the dramatist![32]

If, as Jonson reports, Shakespeare was the first of the "principall Comoedians" of *Every Man in His Humour* in 1598, and one of "the principall Tragoedians" of *Sejanus,* in 1604, then there is no ground for questioning that he was one of the chief actors in *Measure for Measure* when it provided royal entertainment in 1604 at the beginning of the Christmas revels. If, as I have suggested, the play was written not only to amuse the King, but also to show off the acting abilities of several members of the company, and to remind him of other plays he had seen which had been written by their leading playwright, then it would have been a strange oversight indeed if Shakespeare had neglected to provide a part for himself. And what more appropriate than that he should play the part of the Duke, whose abdication sets the play in motion, and whose cleverness brings to a happy ending a plot in which the worst physical and moral evils threaten. With Shakespeare as the Duke, his various styles of speech glance humorously at other plays he has written, and his principles of government can be borrowed out of the King's book without any danger of his seeming to impersonate the King. He is dramatizing the *Basilikon Doron,* making a play of it as William Willymat made a book of epigrams, and Henry Peacham a book of emblems out of it. He is the King's scholar, his puppet, and in the last act he becomes the King's playwright, producing a play which exemplifies the highest ideals of justice and mercy which King James had prescribed for "myself and mine." Seen in this light, the play fits together like a nest of boxes, with Shakespeare, the master-dramatist, directing it as well as acting in it.

Such a view brings us nearer than we have ever been before to the actual production of a Shakespearean play. Here indeed is Greene's "johannes fac totum," acting, directing, and at the end writing as well. It has long been assumed that Shakespeare had something to say about the production of his plays; and that he wrote, especially in the comic parts, with particular actors in mind, but here he is, writing a part for himself—dramatizing himself as playwright, director, and actor.

Once we have recognized Shakespeare in the Duke, the suggestion is inevitable that he also played Prospero, saying at once Prospero's farewell to his magic and Shakespeare's farewell to the stage, and speaking the epilogue in the same meter he had used for the Duke's soliloquy at the end of Act III in *Measure for Measure*. *The Tempest* is also a play written for an occasion, although we do not know the occasion. It seems appropriate for a wedding, and it evidently marked Shakespeare's retirement from his profession as actor. It was performed at court on November 1, 1611.

There is one other play in which we seem to catch a glimpse of Shakespeare in a part similar to that of Duke Vincentio and Duke Prospero: Duke Theseus, in *A Midsummer Night's Dream*, with his wonderful lines on the music of his hounds (IV, i, 123–31) and his playful description (out of Sidney's *Defence of Poesie*) of the poet's art (V, i, 2–22), which would be more effective in Shakespeare's mouth than in any other. And what a delightful situation would be presented by Shakespeare-Theseus patiently enduring while the mechanics make a travesty of a play so suggestive of *Romeo and Juliet*; and then, when they have finished, banishing the mechanics' epilogue and speaking one himself. But, in the absence of further evidence, choosing parts for him becomes an idle game. The very skill with which he created characters, their consistency and plausibility, makes it possible to see him in very many parts. Did he, for example, play Benedick to Burbage's Claudio, and allow himself to be jockeyed into love by his friends, who produced as evidence against him "A halting sonnet of his own pure brain"? The speculation opens new vistas, but it is mere speculation. Unsupported by evidence, it is idle, except as it brings us in some degree, however slight, nearer to the author as he lived and wrote—gives us fresh eyes with which to look at the plays.

X · Conclusions

Shakespeare speaks to each succeeding age in its own idiom because he was more intent to understand than to judge, to express than to evaluate, and more concerned with the enduring than with the temporal in his fellow man. He wrote with charity toward all, and with malice toward none. He was, indeed, for all time, but his own time was one. We have lost much of him in losing the records of that time, and, although the long view which our distance gives us provides perspective and enhances his stature among men, yet ability to see him in his habit as he lived gives freshness and vitality to the view.

Through his plays he speaks directly to the sympathetic understanding, and so forever eludes and baffles his would-be interpreters. He is so much clearer and more widely apprehensible than they. His language, even at its most contorted, has a directness of communication which only dramatic speech can have. Exposition, at best, can merely illuminate the background of time and circumstance, and point to the text. At worst, it can distort and overlay and so obscure that text. However, if the poet's pen can give to his imaginings "a local habitation and a name," so too the interpreter of the poet must, wherever possible, see the play as it lived and moved in performance, in the local habitation of time and place which gave foundation and firm shape to what the poet's imagination bodied forth.

So far as we know now, *Measure for Measure* is unique in providing, in its text, the occasion (confirmed by the record of court performance) and the audience for which it was written.[1] We can see this play as written for the entertainment of King James during the Christmas revels of 1604/5, and from that point of view it becomes a different play from the one known to scholars only as a play written while Shakespeare was preoccupied with tragedies. As a comedy created to entertain the new monarch, it echoes at a polite distance the image which King James instructed his subjects to see in him, and it presents the playwright and his fellow actors in parts designed to show them at their best. Above all, it presents Shakespeare himself, as dramatist, actor, and wit, taking part in a play of his own creating, and, in the last act, planning, directing, and acting the leading part in a play-within-the-play for which the first four acts have been preparation. Moreover, it contains echoes of, or allusions to, other plays by Shakespeare, as well as to the occasion, the King's guest, the Queen's mask, and perhaps to other things about which we know nothing.

We should not, of course, imagine that the performance on December 26, 1604, was the only performance of this play. It was, no doubt, performed on the public stage as a new play in the autumn of 1604; and it was undoubtedly viewed by more than one of the court officials before it was chosen as suitable for the opening of the Christmas festivities on this important occasion. There is no reason to doubt that it remained in the repertory of the company. The peculiar appropriateness to Christmas, even the reference to star and shepherd, have dramatic as well as topical significence. The archetypal pattern of innocence (ignorance of self), learning (through experience of evil), and reform with forgiveness, although it is commemorated at Christmas, is appropriate at any time. We do not suppose that *Twelfth Night* or *Midsummer Night's Dream* were strictly occasional plays, to be acted only on a particular day of the year. *Measure for Measure* is a play appropriate at any season, and in any age, providing we have "placed" it in its Jacobean, its Christian, and its author-actor frame of reference.

Once we see this play in its time, and place, with Shakespeare himself in the stellar role, busy managing his stage puppets, and, in the end, being interrupted and annoyed almost beyond endurance by one of them—once we see the play alive in its moment of time, we have no trouble seeing it not only as pure comedy, but as high comedy, worthy of Matthew Arnold's highest approbation. It lingers in the mind as a Christmas play, as appropriate to its occasion as the *Second Shepherd's Play*, but of a very different order of dramaturgy. The girlish Isabella and the precise Angelo are types of innocents, like Adam and Eve, come into the world (of the play), each failing in the first test and being rescued from the consequences of that failure by Divine Mercy through the human agency of the Duke (*their* creator), who first teaches them true repentance and then forgives, and will guide them in the future (for the Duke has returned).[2] Angelo and Isabella represent the best of mankind, youthful idealists who fail egregiously, "but he that might the vantage best have took found out the remedy." The low-life characters give us the other side of the picture, the worst of humanity: Pompey, the bawd; Lucio, the libertine and libeler; and Mistress Overdone, the professional whore, who are all disciplined, with mercy, by the law; and Barnardine, the lost sheep, who finds a mercy he has not dreamed of. Although the Duke, the key to the whole comedy, is a composite and artificial character, and the action is founded on artifice, the play nevertheless probes truly and deeply, though not solemnly, into the nature of human weakness and limitation.

Once we see this play in its original perspective, we see also implications about other plays. We see Shakespeare as Prospero, and as Duke Theseus. It restores him to his company, and to his quality as actor, sweeping away the ignorant conjectures of Rowe's biography and the fiction that he created, or perpetuated. Biographers have given too much credit to the apocrypha gathered up in the *Shakespeare Allusion-Book*, trying to fit in every detail, as if they were parts of a jigsaw puzzle, every piece authentic.

Seeing *Measure for Measure* no longer as a "splendid failure," but as a comedy no darker than the joyful birth it celebrates—and no more "realistic" than King James's advice to his son!—we are constrained to take a look at that other "dark comedy" which has been described as its obvious twin. G. K. Hunter, in his excellent edition of *All's Well That Ends Well*, says of that play and *Measure for Measure;* "plot, characterization, themes, vocabulary, even the tangles, perplexities, and perversities of treatment [are] shared." [3] Hunter thinks, however, that "what difference there is in these elements points to a slight development and clarification of the material when it is handled in *Measure for Measure*." In other words, he, like most other modern critics, sees *All's Well* (of which no Quarto or record of performance survives) as the earlier play. However, he equates Helena with Isabella as a woman "with clear intelligence and a sense of divine mission" while Isabella is remarkable for "purity of mind and transparent singleness of purpose." [4] If we revise our conception of Isabella to conform more nearly to Shakespeare's representation of her, if we allow Isabella the "innocence" of youth and inexperience, then Helena's heedless pursuit of Bertram differentiates her sharply. Her willingness to stake her virginity and her very life on healing the King (as her only way to get Bertram for a husband) and her equally headlong remorse when she realizes that she has driven him away from home and into danger, her passionate nature and her resourcefulness both mark her as more mature and quite different from Isabella.

Her place in the story parallels that, not of Isabella, but of the rejected Mariana of the moated grange, whom we first see living in nunlike retirement, but still deeply in love with Angelo and willing to do anything to get him for her husband. Shakespeare had no occasion to develop Mariana in *Measure for Measure*. Indeed, he could not give her a third dimension without bringing her into a competition which would have overshadowed the girlish Isabella. For her development he needed another play, and *All's Well* may very well be that later play; but that is another story, to be developed elsewhere.

Having seen one play in its time and place, complete with actors and auditors, we see things hitherto invisible about other plays. We understand and enjoy more richly the last act of *A Midsummer Night's Dream* if we think of Shakespeare as Theseus gravely telling Hippolyta that the adventures "these lovers speak of" are

> More strange than true. I never may believe
> These antic fables nor these fairy toys.

So Sir John Mandeville in his *Travels* assures his readers of the fabulous marvels he is reporting, "I never would have believed it if I had not seen it myself."

>The lunatic, the lover, and the poet
>Are of imagination all compact,

says Theseus, and he goes on to the practical application of what
he is talking about, the "tricks" of "strong imagination," which

>in the night, imagining some fear,
>How easy is a bush supposed a bear!   (V, i, 2–22)

This is prelude to the

>tedious brief scene of young Pyramus
>And his love Thisby; very tragical mirth.

And mirth it is, on the surface as the labored product of "hard-
handed men that work in Athens here," who make a travesty
of their tragedy, and serve as foil to the nobility of Theseus who
"will hear this play,"

>For never anything can be amiss
>When simpleness and duty tender it.

At the same time, and in another context, the play is a parody
of *Romeo and Juliet,* presented for the amusement of the author,
himself (i.e., Duke Theseus). And, in another context, Shakespeare's company, the most polished actors of the day, are doing
a burlesque of amateurs putting on a play. In still another context, Shakespeare-Theseus is taking his cue from the practice
of Queen Elizabeth herself (whom the play assumes as audience),
when he explains to Hippolyta the principle of *noblesse oblige:*

>The kinder we, to give them thanks for nothing.

>   .   .   .

>Where I have come, great clerks have purposèd
>To greet me with premeditated welcomes;
>Where I have seen them shiver and look pale,

> Make periods in the midst of sentences,
> Throttle their practised accent in their fears,
> And, in conclusion, dumbly have broke off . . .
>
> (V, i, 89–105)

This actually happened to Queen Elizabeth more than once. Theseus is speaking, as the Duke does in *Measure for Measure* (I, i, 67–72), sentiments which perfectly express the monarch's attitude, adopted by the stage character as his own, in a kind of imitation which is the purest flattery.

This kind of imitation is on the other side of the world from the imitation which *represents,* whether to mock or flatter. In *A Midsummer Night's Dream,* as in *Measure for Measure,* the playwright assumes the posture of pupil to his monarch. He has learned how a great ruler should act by studying the model set by Elizabeth, or James. He is not a critic (with the assumption of superior judgment which that entails), but a pupil. He learns, not teaches.

Measure for Measure is not a play for the simple, the "identifiers," and the admirers of "realism." Shakespeare's was a highly disciplined and sophisticated age (for those who were educated), where attention to many things at once was a condition of life. The statesman must find his way through a tangled web of plots, lies, private interests and ambitions, and social conventions (including polite lies). He must keep firmly in mind in every act and in every word his own interests and those of his government, the realities of the situation, and the appearances he must present and represent. To such an audience *Measure for Measure* was addressed, an audience capable of enjoying at once the absurdity of Claudio's sentence and his horror of imminent death, the skill of the actor, the polish of his acting, and the eloquence and cleverness of his lines. In this play, more than in any other,

Shakespeare directs attention to the skill of the playwright and to the skill of the actors as conscious art.

It is a witty play, in the Elizabethan sense of "wit." What Shakespeare has done by having the men sentenced to death for adultery and saved by the women is to turn a normal situation upside down, and this paradox (once it is recognized) removes the action from reality as effectively as Prospero's magic wand removes *The Tempest*. Angelo's rectitude is essentially comic. It is pride before the fall. And the ferocity of Claudio's sentence is so exaggerated, in a time when even the Sir Pecksall Brockases are rarely and mildly disciplined, that we should recognize at once that we are in a world of make-believe. The fundamental situation is comic, not because it is fanciful in the manner of *A Midsummer Night's Dream,* but because it paradoxically inverts the accustomed mores. Thereafter the pseudo-serious treatment of the predicament of the seducer and his sister is rendered comic by exaggeration; he is to be executed "tomorrow," she is just entering a nunnery. Even the "realistic underplot" calls attention to its artifice by echoing the Dogberry scenes of *Much Ado,* by reversing the usual London situation where bawdyhouses were frequently ordered pulled down in the City, only to spring up in the suburbs, and by the irony of making Pompey, the professional bawd, reform by becoming bawd to the executioner.

The play is, from beginning to end, pure comedy, based on absurdity, like *The Mikado,* full of topical allusions to a current best seller, and every situation exaggerated into patent theatricality. The great emotional scenes, first Isabella's, then Angelo's, and then Claudio's, each in a different way keep the emotions in check, as they must be kept in check in a comedy, because we cannot be amused when our sympathies are deeply involved. We must feel superior to the foolish people in the play, must know more than they know (or feel that we do), and must be confident that everything will come out right in the end.

The understanding of this multifaceted play restores to us much of the fun of Shakespeare's other comedies. It is not the simple guffaw of the unsophisticated, but the complex enjoyment of many things at once, of the actor as well as of the part he is playing, and here especially of the playwright as the creator of illusions and modulator of emotions.

Moreover, in this play Shakespeare seems to have begun his experiments with the uses of archetypal myth in giving a new dimension of memorability, of depth and serious meaning to a comic plot. Such a suggestion of depth gives a sense of inevitable rightness to the outcome, which justifies, or makes rationally acceptable, all the absurdities and improbabilities of the plot—as, for example, in *The Winter's Tale*. The myth of *Measure for Measure* he found ready to his hand, and to the apprehension of his audience, in the celebration of the coming of Christ. And he gave that story depth, sophistication, and humor by conflating it with King James's account of himself as the earthly representative of God and the ideal ruler. To this "soul," or form, he gave flesh and bone from Whetstone's melodrama, and the result is a polished and many-faceted jewel, dark only in the absence of light. It is a play, not for one occasion, but for many—one too rich in variety of interests to be taken in at one viewing. Like any great work of art, it grows richer with repetition and has something new to offer at each re-viewing.

Notes

CHAPTER I. THE PROBLEM

1. *Shakespeare and His Predecessors* (London, 1896), pp. 344–45.

2. C. J. Sisson, "The Mythical Sorrows of Shakespeare," the Annual Shakespeare Lecture of April 25, 1934, published in the *Proceedings of the British Academy,* Vol. XX, largely demolished this theory. In 1937 R. W. Chambers followed with a solidly documented attack on the notion that Shakespeare was "suffering sorrow and disillusion" and so writing tragedies and bitter comedies in the first decade of the seventeenth century. He demonstrates the general mood of relief and rejoicing created by the peaceful accession of King James; "The Jacobean Shakespeare and 'Measure for Measure'," Annual Shakespeare Lecture, in *Proceedings of the British Academy,* Vol. XXIII, reprinted in *Man's Unconquerable Mind* (London, 1939), pp. 204–49. See also George Gordon, *Shakespearean Comedy* (Oxford, 1945), pp. 41–44, on "Shakespeare's Periods."

3. E. K. Chambers, *Shakespeare: A Survey* (London, 1925), p. 208, n. 4. These essays were first printed between 1904 and 1908; but see also his "Shakespeare, William," *Encyclopaedia Britannica,* 14th edition (1929), XX, 446–47, where Chambers calls it one of "three bitter and cynical pseudo-comedies," "evidence of his profound disillusion and discouragement of spirit."

4. Shakespeare Society, Publications, No. 7, pp. 203–5.

5. *Elizabethan Stage* (Oxford, 1923), IV, 136–41. Chambers gives a clear and concise account of the whole controversy to that date.

6. *Shakespere Forgeries in the Revels Accounts* (New York, 1928). He publishes photographic facsimiles of the pages in question.

7. *William Shakespeare* (Oxford, 1930), II, 330–31.

8. "The Jacobean Shakespeare," p. 54.

9. G. Wilson Knight, in *The Wheel of Fire* (London, 1930), sees the artistic pattern of the play as "tending toward allegory or symbolism" in which "Isabella stands for sainted purity, Angelo for Pharasaical righteousness, the Duke for a psychologically sound and enlightened ethic. Lucio represents indecent wit," etc. I quote the 5th ed. (London, 1962), pp. 73–74. See also Muriel C. Bradbrook, "Authority, Truth and Justice in *Measure for Measure*," *Review of English Studies*, XVII (1941), 385–99, reprinted in *Discussions of Shakespeare's Problem Comedies*, ed. Robert Ornstein (Boston, 1961), pp. 78–87. Miss Bradbrook calls the characters "allegorical rather than symbolical," and suggests that the play might be called "The Contention between Justice and Mercy, or False Authority unmasked by Truth and Humility." Roy Battenhouse explicates *"Measure for Measure* and Christian Doctrine of the Atonement" (*PMLA*, LXI [1946], 1029–59). J. A. Bryant, Jr., surveys several allegorical interpretations and concludes that "Shakespeare . . . here came incredibly close to encompassing the whole scope of man's moral development" (*Hippolyta's View: Some Christian Aspects of Shakespeare's Plays* [University of Kentucky Press, 1961], pp. 86–108). Roland Mushat Frye, in *Shakespeare and Christian Doctrine* (Princeton, 1963), in his first chapter has some devastating critical remarks on the theologizing and allegorizing of Shakespeare's plays, and on p. 94 he singles out *Measure for Measure* as a possible exception (although he is not convinced of it) to his general proposition that "an explicitly New Testament ethic is less relevant to Shakespeare's plays than an ethic of purely natural law, based equally in Scriptures and the Greek and Latin classics." J. Wilson McCutchan,

in "Justice and Equity in the English Morality Play," *Journal of the History of Ideas*, XIX (1958), 405–10, gives a useful sketch of the evolution of these concepts in earlier English drama and jurisprudence. William Nelson, in *The Poetry of Edmund Spenser* (Columbia University Press, 1963), has a useful chapter on Spenser's concept of Justice and Mercy. R. G. Hunter, in *Shakespeare and the Comedy of Forgiveness* (Columbia University Press, 1965), chapter 9, sees the play as a secular discussion of the interdependence of the government of self and of others.

10. *Shakespeare's Problem Comedies* (New York, 1931; reprinted 1959). Lawrence says, "The essential characteristic of a problem play, I take it, is that a perplexing and distressing complication in human life is presented in a spirit of high seriousness" (p. 4); and "The controlling spirit in a problem play must obviously be realism" (p. 7).

11. As early as 1922 Quiller-Couch asked, "What is wrong with this play?" "Introduction" to *Measure for Measure* (*The Works of Shakespeare*, New Cambridge Edition, ed. Sir Arthur Quiller-Couch and John Dover Wilson), p. xiii. He was still under the influence of the "dark period" theory. (See pp. xxii ff.) He concludes that, while Walter Pater was right in considering the idea on which the play is based the idea of Poetic Justice, "the idea has not emerged, because in the author's mind it never attained to being thoroughly clear" (p. xxvii). He finds the basis of the "trouble" in the poet's "failure to make Isabella a consistent character" (p. xxxi).

12. *Shakespeare's Problem Plays* (London, 1950), pp. 2, 3, 5.

13. *Ibid.*, pp. 118–38.

14. *The Problem Plays of Shakespeare* (New York, 1963), p. 6.

15. *As They Liked It* (New York, 1947); and *Shakespeare and the Rival Traditions* (New York, 1952).

16. This Aristotelian concept is discussed by A. C. Bradley, in his *Shakespearean Tragedy* (London, 1904; reprinted 1949), pp. 12 ff. He says, "The centre of the tragedy . . . may be said with equal truth to lie in action issuing from character, or in character

issuing in action." It is the story that makes the character, since only by action (including speech) can character be communicated. However, while Shakespeare began with plot and imagined such characters as might act in that way, yet he sometimes modified a plot to keep his characters, once they had been imagined, consistent.

17. The stage history has been traced by G. C. D. Odell, *Shakespeare from Betterton to Irving*, 2 vols. (London, 1920); Hazleton Spencer, *Shakespeare Improved: The Restoration Versions in Quarto and on the Stage* (Cambridge, 1927); C. B. Hogan, *Shakespeare in the Theatre 1701–1800* (Oxford, 1952); Harold Child, "The Stage History of *Measure for Measure*," in the New Cambridge Edition, pp. 160–65. A. C. Sprague comments on the lack of continuity of the play's history in *Shakespeare and the Actors* (Cambridge, 1945), pp. 64–66.

18. *Johnson: Prose and Poetry*, selected by Mona Wilson (Cambridge, Mass., 1957), p. 538.

19. John Dover Wilson, *The Essential Shakespeare* (Cambridge, 1932), p. 116.

20. E. K. Chambers, *Elizabethan Stage*, IV, 349–50, surveys the records briefly. Lady Hoby reports receiving a list of 31,967 dead in London between July and October. She has heard that they are now counting the living instead of the dead. (*Diary of Lady Margaret Hoby, 1599–1605*, ed. Dorothy M. Meads [Boston, 1930], pp. 204–8.) This is the visitation of the plague commemorated in Thomas Dekker's *The Wonderfull Yeare. 1603.*

21. Before the Queen's funeral, on April 18, precautions were being taken against the plague. With the triple excuse of plague, mourning, and political uncertainty, it is most improbable that playing was resumed in London. A year later, February 8, 1604, the King's Men had a royal warrant for £30 for their relief. Not until March 15, 1604, had the plague sufficiently abated so that the public spectacle of the Coronation procession could be held. (Chambers, *Elizabethan Stage*, IV, 335–36, 349–50.) Chambers suggests that the

theaters may have opened briefly between February 8 and 22 (when Lent began), but he offers no evidence of it. From the terms of the royal gift of February 8 (quoted *ibid.*, IV, 168–69) we learn that the players were prohibited from presenting any plays publicly in or near London "till it shall please God to settle the cittie in a more p'fecte health," so the theaters were certainly not reopened on the 8th. They were reopened on, or shortly after, April 9, 1604, when the Privy Council instructed the Mayor of London and the Justices of Middlesex and Surrey to allow the public playhouses to reopen, "the time of Lent being now Passt." The houses of the King's, Queen's, and Prince's players are specified (*Elizabethan Stage*, IV, 336, 350; see also I, 302). G. B. Harrison, in *A Jacobean Journal* (London, 1941), assumes that the theaters were open in May, 1603, since he places the failure of Jonson's *Sejanus* in that month (see pp. 31–32). The King arrived in London on May 11 and threw himself into the Tower, a choice of residence which astonished the Londoners. The obvious implication was of fear and distrust. On May 19 letters patent were issued to the players to use the Globe "when the infection of the plague shall decrease," and also to play "within anie towne halls or moute halls" in the realm (*Elizabethan Stage*, II, 208). The letters patent were important to establish their legal status so that they could go on tour, and tour they did during the summer of 1603.

22. *Elizabethan Stage*, II, 329, reports a late and uncertain tradition that the play was *As You Like It.*

23. *Elizabethan Stage*, IV, 117–18.

24. Quoted from the *State Papers Domestic, James I* (XII, 19), in Chambers, *William Shakespeare*, II, 332; and see *Elizabethan Stage*, IV, 139.

25. *Elizabethan Stage*, IV, 171; and see the "Court Calendar," on p. 119.

26. John Chamberlain wrote to Winwood on January 26, 1605, "The Kinge went to Roiston two dayes after Twelfetide" (*Letters of John Chamberlain*, ed. N. E. McClure [Philadelphia, 1939], I, 201).

His absence accounts for the entertainment of the Queen and most of the court elsewhere, since her brother, the Duke of Holst, was her guest.

27. *Measure for Measure* (New Cambridge Ed.), pp. 101–3.

28. *Ben Jonson,* ed. C. H. Herford, and Percy and Evelyn Simpson (Oxford, 1925–52), X, 445–49. Chamberlain reported on December 18 that £3000 had been paid "a month ago" (*Letters,* I, 198). See also *Stage,* III, 375–77; and the letter of December 5, from Thomas Edmondes to the Earl of Shrewsbury reporting the cost (E. Lodge, *Illustrations of British History* [London, 1791], III, 250). On December 12 John Packer wrote to Winwood particulars about the women who were to take part (Sir Ralph Winwood, *Memorials of Affairs of State* [London, 1725], II, 39–40, 41).

29. John Nichols, *The Progresses, Processions, and Magnificent Festivities of King James the First* (London, 1828), I, 468–74. *Elizabethan Stage,* III, 375–77, reports some of the gossip and scandals of the performance.

30. I quote from the Pelican Shakespeare, *Measure for Measure* ed. R. C. Bald (Baltimore, 1956), throughout. The Arden Shakespeare, *Measure for Measure,* ed. S. W. Lever (London and Cambridge, Mass., 1965) did not appear in time for use.

31. Ben Jonson, in his Preface to the Quarto, says that he created the mask because "It was her majesty's will to have them *Blackmoors* at first" (*Jonson,* II, 265). E. K. Chambers, in *Shakespeare,* I, 453, questions the allusion, saying, "but although the maskers entered in a shell ['enshelled' F. 'en-shield'] they were painted black and wore no masks." Surely the black paint was a mask, i.e., covering to disguise the face. Moreover, "Black masks" is a clear allusion to, and pun on, the name "Masque of Blackness." Inigo Jones created a huge shell, lined with mother-of-pearl, in which the black-faced maskers (the Queen and eleven of her ladies) made their entrance.

32. Dover Wilson (New Cambridge Ed., pp. 104–7) identifies this as a reference to the peace made by the empire with the Turks, November 11, 1606, which handed over 700 villages and some for-

tified towns to the Turks. It was signed by the King of Hungary. He uses this identification to argue that the play performed at court in 1604 was revised, and a cut-down version prepared for court performance after November, 1606.

33. Chamberlain to Winwood (*Letters,* I, 198).

34. The Queen was expecting a child in April. The Duke stayed for the christening (Nichols, *Progresses,* I, 466, 515). The Queen's pregnancy was known as early as October 3 (*Ibid.,* I, 459).

35. Henry Chettle, in *England's Mourning Garment* (1603), prays for the unity of Christendom, "the better [to] be repelled from those wealthy Kingdomes in the East [the heathen]." He says that the blood shed in religious wars in the last thirty years is enough "to have driven the heathen Monarch from his neerest holde in Hungarie, to the fal of Danubia in the Euxine sea" (Sig. B4). On November 14 the Earl of Shrewsbury wrote to Lord Lumley, "The Queen's Brother is come to Court, but not very rytche eny way" (Nichols, *Progresses,* I, 466). For a sketch of the situation in Hungary see *The Cambridge Modern History,* ed. A. W. Ward, *et al.,* III (Cambridge, 1904), 684, 700–3, 720–22, 777; and F. F. Roget, "The Huguenots of Hungary," *Proceedings of the Huguenot Society of London,* XIII (1925), 98–104.

36. See below, chapter VI.

37. Lawrence, in *Shakespeare's Problem Comedies,* pp. 79 ff., argues that Isabella's dilemma "may apparently be ultimately traced to an episode in real life. . . . It is a human problem; there is nothing about it which is illogical or unbelievable."

38. Geoffrey Bullough, in *Narrative and Dramatic Sources of Shakespeare,* II (London and New York, 1958), 399 ff., gives an adequate account of the many analogues which have been cited, though, curiously enough, he does not mention the story of Abram and Sarai in Egypt: Genesis 12: 5–20.

39. Wilson, in "The Copy for *Measure for Measure,* 1623" (New Cambridge Ed., pp. 97–113), argues for more than one revision, but his evidence is unconvincing.

CHAPTER II. THE PLOT

1. H. C. Hart, editor of this play in the Arden *Shakespeare*, XXII (1905), xiii–xxi, reviews the sources and analogues. Mary Lascelles, in *Shakespeare's Measure for Measure* (London, 1953), discusses the sources at length. Madeleine Doran, in *Endeavors in Art* (Madison, Wis., 1954), pp. 385–89, reviews the sources and argues for Cintio's *Epitia* as one of them. Kenneth Muir, in *Shakespeare's Sources* (London, 1957), presents a brief survey. Bullough, in *Sources* II, 399–530, reprints most of the sources.

2. Bullough reprints this play, but not Whetstone's summary of it, in the *Heptameron*. In "The Printer to the Reader" the play (or plays) is described as a "fyrst copy" which the author had no time to polish, and in the *Heptameron* Whetstone says that it has "never yet been presented on the stage."

3. Bullough, *Sources*, II, 400; F. E. Budd, "Rouillet's *Philanira* and Whetstone's *Promos and Cassandra*," *Review of English Studies*, VI (1930), 31–48; and "Materials for the Study of the Sources of Shakespeare's *Measure for Measure*," *Revue de Littérature Comparée* (1931), pp. 711–36.

4. Bullough, *Sources*, II, 405–6. Recently Charles T. Prouty has suggested further sources, in "George Whetstone and the Sources of *Measure for Measure*," *Shakespeare Quarterly*, XV (No. 2, 1964), 131–45.

5. Bullough, *Sources*, II, 406. R. G. Hunter, in *Shakespeare and the Comedy of Forgiveness*, pp. 209–13, has a useful discussion of Elizabethan concern about adultery, chiefly from sermons.

6. The failure of the punishment to fit the crime troubled R. W. Chambers, who said (*Man's Unconquerable Mind*, p. 284) "This Viennese law seems strange, but . . . . It is a postulate of the story." W. W. Lawrence says, "We do not need to take this 'statute' too seriously; law in Shakespeare's plays is queer business. The important thing to note is that the usage in England in Shakespeare's day was

that here represented as the common custom in Vienna, before the reform instituted by Angelo" (*Shakespeare's Problem Comedies,* p. 97).

7. See I, ii, 140–42.

8. See the article on "Marriage" in the *Encyclopaedia Britannica* 11th ed., sections on "canon law" and "England"; C. L. Powell, *English Domestic Relations, 1487–1653* (New York, 1917), "Introduction." Spousals *de praesenti,* including the secret exchange of vows, although disapproved by both the church and state, were held by both to be binding. "They are very man and wife before God." See Claudio's "She is fast my wife" (I, ii, 142).

9. See E. K. Chambers, *Shakespeare,* I, 17–18, and II, 41–52; and J. Q. Adams, *Life of William Shakespeare* (Boston, 1923), pp. 67–78.

10. Leslie Hotson, *I William Shakespeare* (New York, 1938), pp. 138–40, 203 ff. Russell was named overseer of Shakespeare's will.

11. Sir Richard Baker, *Chronicle of the Kings of England* (London, 1643), p. 140. This entry does not give the year, but it is placed between entries for 1609 and 1614. Baker was knighted by King James in 1603. He is evidently writing of this remarkable occurrence from memory.

12. Malone Society, *Collectanea,* Vol. I, Pt. 2 (1908), p. 161. It should be noted that in both cases ecclesiastical authorities are involved. Shakespeare makes a comic reversal of the usual custom when he has Pompey report a proclamation that "All houses in the suburbs of Vienna must be plucked down" while those in the city "shall stand for seed; they had gone down too, but that a wise burgher put in for them" (I, ii, 92–97). In London it was the City which was severe; the suburbs (and the "liberties") afforded refuge.

13. Every critic has followed Coleridge in denouncing Angelo as a monster, and Shakespeare, for allowing him to be forgiven.

14. The whole basis for considering the first half of the play as "realistic" is the assumption that Isabella has a real dilemma, that

she actually makes a choice. W. W. Lawrence, *Shakespeare's Problem Comedies*, pp. 4–7, 79, and *passim*, insists on the realism of the play. Tillyard, *Shakespeare's Problem Plays*, pp. 118–38, accepts Lawrence's view for the first half of the play, but not for the second half.

15. *Man's Unconquerable Mind*, pp. 300 ff.

16. See above, ch. I, n. 9. All of the allegorizers have caught a glimpse of this meaning, but they have tried to make it too specific, too theological and allegorical, not simply the primeval story pattern with allusions.

17. Roy Battenhouse ("*Measure for Measure* and Christian Doctrine of the Atonement," *PMLA*, LXI [1946], p. 1038, n. 29) cites Romans 13: 11–12, "It is time for you to awake out of sleep: for now is salvation nearer to us than we first believed. The night is far spent, the day is at hand." J. A. Bryant, Jr., in *Hippolyta's View*, pp. 105–7, notes that this chapter of Romans was read in both Roman and Anglican Uses at the beginning of Advent. It was especially emphasized in Elizabethan times because it enjoined obedience to rulers as "God's ministers," and love of thy neighbor as fulfillment of God's law. Bishop Hooper required the teaching of it in his diocese every week. Whether or not Shakespeare had this chapter specifically in mind, it affords in brief the whole meaning of the Nativity, or Advent, as the Elizabethans understood it. Bryant sees the story of Claudio, Isabella, and Angelo as the story of *humanum genus*: "The stage whereon man falls from grace, comes to know himself under the dispensation of the Mosaic law, and finds redemption at last under the dispensation of grace with the return of his Lord in the full light of morning."

18. Walter Raleigh, in *Shakespeare* (New York, 1907), pp. 148–49, calls Barnardine a "perfect gratuity," since "the plot is managed without him." Lascelles discusses him inconclusively (*Shakespeare's Measure for Measure*, pp. 108–13).

19. Lawrence (*Shakespeare's Problem Comedies*, p. 89) speaks of "the vivid picture of sexual impurity in Vienna"; L. C. Knights

begins with the statement, "the mainspring of the action is, of course, the sexual instinct" ("The Ambiguity of *Measure for Measure,*" reprinted from *Scrutiny,* X [1942], 222–34, in *The Importance of Scrutiny,* ed. Eric Bentley [New York, 1948], pp. 141–50).

20. *Basilikon Doron* (London, 1603), p. 76.

21. See below, ch. VI, n. 39.

22. Nichols, *Progresses, Processions, and Magnificent Festivities of King James the First* (London, 1828), I, 459; and see John Chamberlain's *Letters* (Philadelphia, 1939), I, 198.

23. John Donne, in his "Divine Poems," plays with the paradoxes of the first and second Adam, and calls the Virgin Mary "The Maker's maker, and thy Father's mother" (*The Poems of John Donne,* ed. W. J. C. Grierson [Oxford, 1912], I, 319 ff.).

24. Battenhouse, "*Measure for Measure* and Christian Doctrine of the Atonement," *PMLA,* LXI (1946), 1029–59.

25. Arthur Wilson, *The History of Great Britain, Being The Life and Reign of King James the First* (London, 1653), p. 8; and see below, ch. VI and *passim.*

CHAPTER III. THE PLEASURE OF ART

1. "Astrophil and Stella," *The Poems of Sir Philip Sidney,* ed. W. A. Ringler, Jr. (Oxford, 1962), p. 165. Sonnet 2 opens: "Not at first sight, nor with a dribbed shot/*Love* gave the wound, which while I breathe will bleed:" The Quartos read "dribbing." The use of this distinctive word makes the allusion obvious, and Shakespeare's interpretation of it is therefore significant.

2. The attacks on the character of the Duke are much concerned with the propriety of his disguise and his usurpation of the religious function of hearing confessions, but disguise as a friar was convenient, and therefore common as a stage convention; the Anglican and Jamesian concept of the ruler as God's representative made it appropriate (see below, ch. VI); he does not administer sacraments, or otherwise function as a priest; he says that he has confessed Mariana

and Angelo, but about Angelo, at least, the audience knows that he is lying; and his "consolation" of Claudio, out of mediaeval *contemptu mundi* treatises, is appropriate to his Friar's garb, but old fashioned, extended to absurdity, and therefore comic. The Duke is talking like a mediaeval friar, i.e., playing a part.

3. Warren D. Smith could find no case of nonroyal use of the plural pronoun in Shakespeare except this one (II, iv, 185) and one in which Julius Caesar betrays his ambition (*Julius Caesar*, III, i, 8); see "More Light on *Measure for Measure*," *Modern Language Quarterly*, XXIII (1962), 309–22.

4. R. W. Chambers (*Man's Unconquerable Mind*, pp. 204–49) makes the most extravagant defense of Isabella, and Sir Arthur Quiller-Couch the most virulent attack ("Introduction" to the New Cambridge Edition, pp. xxvii-xxxiii).

5. Quiller-Couch, *ibid.*, p. xxxix, says, "The two halves of this scene cannot be made of a piece by anyone possessing even a rudimentary acquaintance with English prose and poetry." He says it was not written "at one spell, on one inspiration, or with anything like an identical or even continuous poetic purpose." I believe that the contrast is deliberate, and dramatically very effective. See below, ch. VIII.

6. Tillyard calls it a "splendid failure" (*Shakespeare's Problem Plays*, p. 142) because of this break; and see pp. 123, 139–42. K. Muir agrees that the play falls into two parts (*Shakespeare's Sources*, p. 108). O. J. Campbell, in *Shakespeare's Satire* (Oxford, 1943), pp. 121–41, attributes faults in the structure to the over-characterization of Isabella. V. K. Whitaker says that it is "patched up" and "The result was simply confusion"; see "Philosophy and Romance in Shakespeare's 'Problem' Comedies," *The Seventeenth Century: Studies by R. F. Jones and Others* (Stanford, Calif., 1951), p. 354. T. M. Parrott calls the play "by no means a triumph of Shakespeare's art"; see *Shakespearean Comedy* (New York, 1949), pp. 364–65. R. M. Smith gives a useful survey of critical judgments in "Interpretations of *Measure for Measure*," *Shakespeare Quarterly*,

I (1950), 208–18. W. D. Smith treats the whole play as realistic and reconciles all character changes by the argument that they are "dynamic" ("More Light on *Measure for Measure*," *Modern Language Quarterly*, XXIII [1962], 309–22).

7. The Duke's motive has been questioned because he hands over his authority to Angelo when he must already have known of Angelo's treatment of Mariana, but this is false reasoning in two respects. Angelo's behavior is not illegal, nor even immoral. It is merely practical (she has lost her dowry) and cold-hearted. In the second place, it is false analysis of a play to require a knowledge revealed in Act III to be taken into account in Act I. The conditions of theatrical representation, with linear progression and imprecise tempo, make such real-life requirements absurd.

8. See W. W. Lawrence, *Shakespeare's Problem Comedies,* pp. 94–102. It is curious that in discussing this method of getting a husband no one seems to have mentioned the precedent of Leah and Rachel.

9. Dover Wilson describes the passage as misplaced and evidence of hasty revision; see New Cambridge ed., p. 98. Quiller-Couch (*ibid.*, p. xxxix) would add these six lines to the end of III, ii, 178–81, because they are on the same subject!

10. D. L. Stevenson, in "Design and Structure in *Measure for Measure*: a New Appraisal," *ELH,* XXIII (1956), 262 f., makes this point well.

11. See below, ch. VI.

12. See below, ch. V, p. 73.

CHAPTER IV. PARADOX, MACABRE HUMOR,
AND SUSPENSE

1. *The Complete Plays and Poems of William Shakespeare,* ed. W. A. Neilson and C. J. Hill, The New Cambridge Edition (Cambridge, Mass., 1942), p. 518. This text has been used for all quotations except for *Measure for Measure* and *Much Ado about Nothing*.

CHAPTER V. ISABELLA

1. Bullough, *Sources*, II, 408. Angelo's demand is outrageous whether or not Isabella is a novice; it is outrageous with or without "supernatural injunctions." Just how she can "transcend the part she has henceforth to play" is beyond my comprehension, but Shakespeare's "hesitation" is not apparent. He very much more than "hints" at the Duke's proposal. In fact, the Duke proposes twice, using traditional formulas both times. Sir Arthur Quiller-Couch thinks that she should have returned to her nunnery ("Introduction" to the New Cambridge ed., p. xxxi). R. W. Chambers calls such critics "more Papistical than the Pope" (*Man's Unconquerable Mind*, pp. 306–7). W. W. Lawrence refuses to see anything scandalous in the marriage of Isabella to the Duke (*Shakespeare's Problem Comedies*, pp. 106–7).

2. "Introduction" to the New Cambridge Edition, p. xxx.

3. E. K. Chambers, *Shakespeare: A Survey*, p. 215. R. W. Chambers agrees.

4. Lawrence, *Shakespeare's Problem Comedies*, p. 79.

5. *Shakespeare's Problem Plays*, pp. 127–28.

6. This is a famous principle of Queen Elizabeth, who insisted that her subjects be called to account only for their deeds, not for their thoughts. It is interesting to find Shakespeare putting these words into the mouth of Isabella—expressing a principle which barred the Inquisition from England, and compulsory confession from Anglicanism.

7. Deut. 19: 21, and Exod. 21: 23–24, referred to in Matt. 5: 38.

8. Matt. 7: 1–2, and see the Lord's Prayer, Matt. 6: 12, 14–15, and also Luke 6: 35–37.

9. *Basilikon Doron* (1603), p. 7.

10. *Man's Unconquerable Mind*, p. 307.

11. Lawrence, in *Shakespeare's Problem Comedies*, pp. 106–7, is

clear and sound on this point. Muriel C. Bradbrook, in "Authority, Truth and Justice in *Measure for Measure*," *Review of English Studies*, XVII (1941), 385–99, confuses traditional symbolism when she calls Isabella "the bride of the Church." The usual interpretation of The Canticles identifies the bridegroom as Christ, and the church as his bride. Nuns are frequently called "brides of Christ."

12. Quiller-Couch speaks of "her novitiate head-dress" ("Introduction" to the New Cambridge Edition, p. xxxi).

CHAPTER VI. THE DUKE

1. *Shakespeare's Problem Comedies*, p. 110.

2. Edmund Malone credited Thomas Tyrwhitt with this observation (*Boswell's Malone* [1821, "Life," II, 383 f.]). E. K. Chambers is inclined to discredit the evidence of the two proclamations usually cited, on the ground that they were precautions against the plague (*Shakespeare*, I, 453). But there is much other evidence. Chamberlain says of his hunting at Roiston, "Though he seeke to be very private and retired where he is. . . ." And he reports the King's request to his council that he "be not interrupted nor troubled with too much business" (*Letters*, I, 201). Arthur Wilson, in *The History of Great Britain being the Life and Reign of James the First* (1653), p. 3, says, "The King as unused, so tired with *Multitudes*, especially in his *Hunting* . . . caused an inhibition to be published, to restrain the people from *Hunting* him." Again Wilson writes (p. 12), "he did not *love* to be looked on," "these *formalities* of State, which set a *lustre* upon *Princes* in the peoples eyes, were but so many burdens to him . . . . when he came abroad, he was so troubled with *swarms*, that he feared to be baited by the *people*. He was not like his predecessor. . . ." And of the coronation procession, "He endured the *days* brunt with *patience*, being assured he should never have such another . . . but afterwards in his *publick* appearances (especially in his *sports*) the accesses of the people made him so impatient, that he often dispersed them with *frowns*, that we may not

say with *curses*. . . ." Before he left Scotland, on April 5, he began issuing proclamations to stop "the overmuch resort of people to the King." He forbade common people from entering the park at Windsor "on account of injury done to the game," and he forbade any persons except those appointed by him to enter the Privy Chamber (Nos. 959 and 964 of the "Bibliography of Royal Proclamations," Vol. I, ed. Robert Steele [Oxford, 1910], in Vol. V of *Bibliotheca Lindsiana*).

3. Nichols, *Progresses*, I, 188.

4. George Chalmers quoted this report in *A Supplemental Apology for the Believers in the Shakespeare-Papers* (1799), pp. 406–8, which speaks of "his desire to withdraw himself, from places of most access, and company, to places of more solitude, and repose, with very small retinue. . . ."

5. Gilbert Dugdale's *The Time Triumphant . . . His Coronation* (1604), noticed by D. L. Stevenson, "The Role of James I in Shakespeare's *Measure for Measure*," *ELH*, XXVI (1959), 188–208; see pp. 191–92.

6. Thomas Dekker, "To the Reader," *The Magnificent Entertainment* (1604), p. 24; quoted in *Ben Jonson*, ed. C. H. Herford and Percy and Evelyn Simpson, X (Oxford, 1941), 387.

7. See n. 5 above.

8. *Ben Jonson*, VII, 115.

9. *Neue Untersuchungen zu Shakespeares Mass für Mass* (Berlin), pp. 129–244. Unfortunately, Dr. Albrecht depended upon Sir Walter Scott's novel, *The Fortunes of Nigel*, for evidence of the character of King James.

10. See n. 5 above.

11. Mary Lascelles, in *Shakespeare's Measure for Measure*, p. 109, dismisses the idea: "It is surely time that we heard the last of that supposed connection between the Duke's sagacity, and *Basilikon Doron*." W. W. Lawrence, in *Shakespeare's Problem Comedies*, p. 108, finds "little ground for thinking that James I lent . . . more than a touch or two, at most, and none whatsoever that Shakespeare

utilized the *Basilikon Doron* for his play." K. Muir, in *Shakespeare's Sources*, I, 101–10, does not mention it. G. Bullough, in *Narrative and Dramatic Sources of Shakespeare*, II, 397–530, ignores it, as do modern editions and most discussions of the play. Recently C. T. Prouty suggested that the Duke's principles of government derived from some works of George Whetstone's ("Whetstone and the Sources of *Measure for Measure*," *Shakespeare Quarterly*, XV, no. 2 [1964], 131–45).

12. James Craigie edited it for The Scottish Text Society, 2 vols. (1944, 1950). See Vol. II, pp. 22–26.

13. Chamberlain had heard of it by October 15, 1602, as a work of the King of Scots which was about to be printed, and on March 30, 1603, he sent a copy to Carleton (*Letters*, I, 167, 191).

14. W. A. Jackson, *Records of the Court of the Stationers' Company 1602–1640* (London, 1957), pp. 2–3, 5.

15. *Ibid.*, p. 3, note. White, who had 500 copies of Allde's second printing, and had sold them, was also fined (*ibid.*, p. 3). Pavier was fined for selling 75 copies (*ibid.*, p. 4, note). *The Short Title Catalogue*, ed. A. W. Pollard and G. R. Redgrave (London, 1926), records six editions, nos. 14349–54 for 1603; but the Folger Shakespeare Library records three editions under 14350, two under 14351, and three under 14353. Number 14354 is by "E. Allde for E. W. and others of the Company of Stationers, 1603." We know that there were two unauthorized printings by Allde, and Jackson's note refers to printers other than Allde.

16. *Works of Francis Bacon*, ed. James Spedding, R. L. Ellis, and D. D. Heath, VI (London, 1858), 278–79. The passage occurs at the end of a few pages of *The Beginning of the History of Great Britain*, written about 1610, a fragment entirely concerned with the reasons for King James's easy and peaceful accession to the English throne.

17. "A Panegyrike Congratulatorie Delivered to the Kings most excellent Maiestie at Burleigh Harrington in Rutlandshire." It was published, with "certaine Epistles, with *A Defence of Ryme* hereto-

fore written" (1603); reprinted in *The Complete Works of Samuel Daniel,* ed. A. B. Grosart (London, 1885), I, 143–67. See stanzas 20–31.

18. *Ben Jonson,* VII, 116, ll. 113–27. For notes on the *Panegyre,* published in 1604 along with the text of Jonson's part of the coronation pageantry, see Vol. VII, pp. 67–79.

19. *The History of . . . Princess Elizabeth,* 4th ed. (1688), p. 564.

20. Craigie, in *Basilikon Doron,* II, 22–54. He also (pp. 54–62) traces its decline in reputation after 1688.

21. *Academiae Oxoniensis Pietas* (Oxford, 1603), pp. 6, 8; and *Sorrowes Joy,* the Cambridge tribute, reprinted in Nichols, *Progresses,* I, 1–24.

22. G. Pellegrini, *John Florio e il Basilicon Doron di James VI* (Milan, 1961). He prints Florio's translation with a useful introduction sketching Continental interest in the book.

23. The manuscript has been preserved. The 1612 volume, *Minerva Britanna,* prints both the Latin and English, mixing in other emblems. The author describes his labors in his dedication to Prince Henry. The *Basilikon Doron* continued to be read throughout the reign. James Cleland quotes it frequently in *Hro-Paideia, or the Instruction of a Young Nobleman* (1607). Patrick Scot pays homage to it in *Omnibus et Singularis* (1619), translated under the title *A Fathers Advice, or Last Will to his Son* (1620); and in his *Table-Book for Princes* (1621). Sir John Stradling cites it in his *Beati Pacifici* (1623). Sir Henry Saville refers to it in dedicating to the King his learned edition of the *Works* of St. John Chrysostom. Bacon makes reference to it in *The Advancement of Learning,* Book II, and also in *De Augmentis Scientiarum,* Book VII, ch. 2. Robert Burton speaks of the *Basilikon Doron* in his elegy for James in *The Anatomy of Melancholy.* Thomas Fuller, in his *Holy and Profane States* (1642), commends it in Bk. IV, ch. 19, Max. 5, and elsewhere. Craigie analyzes several of these references in his edition of *Basilikon Doron,* II, 39–62. C. H. McIlwain, *The Political Works of*

James I (Cambridge, Mass., 1918), reprints the work and discusses its political theory; and see C. J. Sisson, "King James the First of England as Poet and Political Writer," in *Seventeenth Century Studies Presented to Sir Herbert Grierson* (Oxford, 1938), pp. 47–63.

24. I quote from the Folger Shakespeare Library copy no. 14353, "Imprinted by Richard Field for Iohn Norton according to the Copie printed at Edenburgh. 1603"; see sig. B3ᵛ, at the end of the Address to the Reader.

25. Craigie, in the Commentary to his edition, II, 39–42, collects King James's references to it; and see Sisson, "King James the First," in *Seventeenth Century Studies*.

26. *Measure for Measure*, III, ii, 244–53. D. L. Stevenson, in "The Role of James I in Shakespeare's *Measure for Measure*," ELH, XXVI, p. 199, cites the opening of *Basilikon Doron*.

27. Craigie, II, 63–87, reviews the book's literary antecedents; and see Elizabeth M. Pope, "The Renaissance Background of *Measure for Measure*," *Shakespeare Survey*, II (Cambridge, 1949), 66–82, for further parallels.

28. L. Albrecht, *Neue Untersuchungen zu Shakespeares Mass für Mass*, p. 201.

29. *Ibid.*, 204–16. See also Norman Nathan, "The Marriage of Duke Vincentio and Isabella," *Shakespeare Quarterly*, VII (1956), 43–45.

30. Sig. A1ᵛ. In this passage the King is more emphatic: "For Kings being publicke persons, by reason of their office and authoritie, are as it were set (as it was sayd of old) vpon a publique stage, in the sight of all the people; where all the beholders eyes are attentivelie bent," etc.

31. *Ben Jonson*, VII, 115.

32. *Basilikon Doron*, pp. 41–42, and see p. 52, p. 6, and A2ᵛ ff., A5ᵛ ff., etc.

33. *Ibid.*, Sig. A2ᵛ.

34. H. Chettle, *Englandes Mourning Garment*, Sig. B1ᵛ, B2.

35. *Basilikon Doron*, Sig. A3. Craigie, in Vol. I, prints both the 1599 and the 1603 texts, in parallel. Comparison of the two shows that the King did not soften but rather amplified his remarks about the Puritans, by whom he says he means not only the Anabaptists and the Family of Love, but all those who attack kings in "divers famous libels, & injurious speaches spred by some of them, not onely dishonourably invective against all Christian princes, but even reprochefull to our profession and religion." Sig. A5ᵛ. See also pp. 39 ff.

36. *Basilikon Doron*, p. 42.

37. *Ibid.*, p. 52.

38. *Ibid.*, p. 92.

39. The report sent to Queen Elizabeth in 1586 contains the phrases, "the report is of those, who are nearest about him, very chast, and yet desirous of marriage" (Chalmers, *Suppl. Apology*, p. 408). Sir John Davies, in the dedication of his *Scourge of Folly*, calls him "For Bounty, Clemency, and Chastity preeminent." Sir Richard Baker, who was knighted by King James in 1603, says, "Of all the Morrall vertues, he was eminent for chastity; in which the Poet seemes to include all vertue, where he saith: Nulli fas casto sceleratum in sistere lumen. By nulli casto meaning no vertuous person." He also reports that James challenged comparison with Queen Elizabeth in this virtue (*Chronicle*, p. 155). James's fondness for young men is sufficiently notorious.

40. *Measure for Measure*, IV, iii, 174. The figure of speech may be an allusion to the thistle of Scotland.

41. See above, ch. II. This was one of the many knights created by the King on his way to London. Other references to him, in letters of the period, seem to indicate that he was unworthy of the rank.

42. For the King's advice to his son to be chaste, see *Basilikon Doron*, pp. 73–76.

43. *Ibid.*, pp. 24–26.

44. *Ibid.*, p. 29.

45. *Ibid.*, pp. 30–31. Stevenson ("The Role of James I," *ELH*, XXVI, 188–208) notes many of these parallels.

46. *Ibid.*, p. 25.

47. *Ibid.*, p. 43.

48. *Ibid.*, p. 67.

49. *Ibid.*, pp. 23[misfolioed 32]–24, and see pp. 60, 83–84.

50. *Ibid.*, p. 5.

51. *Ibid.*, p. 61.

52. *Ibid.*, pp. 90, 92.

53. Mary Lascelles, "Sir Thomas Elyot and the Legend of Alexander Severus," *Review of English Studies*, New Series, II (1951), 305–18; and *Shakespeare's Measure for Measure*, p. 101. She traces Elyot's use of this legend in *The Image of Governance* and the *Dictionary*, and in Whetstone's *Mirour for Magistrates of Cyties* (1584), unsold sheets of which were issued as *The Enemie of Unthryftinesse* in 1586. O. J. Campbell, in *Shakespeare's Satire*, p. 127, calls attention to Marston's repeated use of a disguised Duke in three plays of 1599–1602.

54. See Percy M. Thornton, *The Stuart Dynasty* (London, 1890), pp. 119–23, for James V's disguise as the "Goodman of Ballengiech," his designation "King of the Commons," and his courting in disguise of Marie de Bourbon and falling in love with the Princess Madeleine whom he married.

55. He tells Prince Henry: "remember of the honourable stile giuen to my grand-father of worthy memorie, in being called *the poore mans King*" (*Basilikon Doron*, p. 35).

56. E. K. Chambers, in *Shakespeare*, I, 467–76, puts *King Lear* before *Macbeth*. *Lear* was entered in the *Stationers' Register* on November 26, 1607, as acted at court on St. Stephen's night "at Christmas Last," i.e., December 26, 1606. *Macbeth* was not printed until 1623, but the possibly topical references of IV, i, 121, and IV, iii, 141, could have been written as early as 1604. Since the play is so clearly written for King James, it is tempting to see it as

the dramatist's offering of 1605/6, as *Measure for Measure* was in 1604/5, and *Lear* in 1606/7.

57. Stevenson, "The Role of James I," *ELH*, XXVI, 304–6; and see Robert Cecil's letter of December 12, in Ralph Winwood, *Memorials of Affairs of State* (London, 1725), II, 10–11, where he speaks of "the excellent Mixture of the King's Mercy with Justice." Albrecht, in *Neue Untersuchungen*, pp. 181–86, instances the King's crafty dealing with Raleigh; and see the papers on John Ogleby's mission to Spain, in Winwood, *Memorials*, I, 2 ff. and 51–52.

58. See below, ch. VII. The official version was written by King James, and he suppressed all other witnesses. Queen Elizabeth's ambassador thought the King had conspired to slay the Gowries, and he reports that that was the general opinion; see Samuel Cowan, *The Gowrie Conspiracy: and Its Official Narrative* (London, 1902), pp. 7–18, 116–18.

59. *Basilikon Doron*, p. 88.

60. *Ibid.*, p. 153.

61. *Ibid.*, pp. 85, 86.

62. *Ibid.*, p. 92, and Stevenson, "The Role of James I," *ELH*, XXVI, 204.

63. Stevenson, pp. 199–200, cites some of the adulation of James as a "philosopher king" in 1603 and later. The Greek title chosen for this book of advice to his son is one of many evidences of his vanity on this point.

64. *Basilikon Doron*, pp. 3–12, 89–90.

65. *Ibid.*, pp. 54, 60.

66. *Ibid.*, pp. 88–94.

67. *Ibid.*, pp. 85–88. The King advises the use of temperance repeatedly, and other often repeated precepts are, "Do as you would be done by," and "set a good example to your people"; nor does he hesitate to advise, "follow my example."

68. Stevenson, "The Role of James I," *ELH*, XXVI, 207.

69. See the quotation from W. W. Lawrence at the beginning of this chapter.

70. Rufus Cole, *Human History: The Seventeenth Century and the Stuart Family* (Freeport, Maine, 1959), p. 254; and see pp. 318–19 on his appearance and character.

71. *Studies in Shakespeare* (1849), p. 319, quoting Chalmers.

72. *Pace* Leslie Hotson, *The First Night of* Twelfth Night (New York, 1954). E. K. Chambers, in *Elizabethan Stage,* I, 223 f., gives a general account of the selection of plays. Bernard Beckerman, in *Shakespeare at the Globe: 1599–1609* (New York, 1962), pp. 20–21, lists seven plays definitely and one "probably" opened at court. All seven were presented after Shakespeare's time. For the doubtful one we have record of a payment for preparation of *As Merry as May Be* for court performance in mid-November. This company (the Admiral's) played at court on December 27, March 6, and possibly March 8, 1602–3. Whether any of these plays was *As Merry as May Be* we do not know, but even if it was the December 27th play, there was plenty of time to try it out in the usual playing place of the company—and no reason to suppose that it was not so tried out.

73. See below, ch. VII, for documentation.

CHAPTER VII. THE KING AND THE KING'S PLAYERS

1. See above, ch. VI, p. 85.

2. From Isocrates' *Ad Demonicum.* See my article in the *Shakespeare Quarterly,* IV (1953), 3–9.

3. See my article, "Jacques' Seven Ages," *The Shakespeare Association Bulletin,* XVIII (1943), 168–74, tracing Shakespeare's images to a dictionary, the *Onomasticon* of Julius Pollux, in R. Gualther's Latin translation. S. C. Chew, in *The Pilgrimage of Life* (New Haven, 1962), pp. 163–69, traces the pictorial tradition.

4. *Letters,* I, 199.

5. E. K. Chambers, *Elizabethan Stage,* IV, 332, notes a play at the Curtain in 1601 to which the Privy Council objected because it represented on the stage "some gentlemen of good desert and quality that are yet alive." We know that Sir John Oldcastle had to be rechris-

tened Falstaff because Lord Brook objected to Shakespeare's representation of his ancestor, who had been dead for over 150 years.

6. Chambers, *Elizabethan Stage*, III, 275–76. Laurence Michel, in his edition, *The Tragedy of Philotas by Samuel Daniel* (New Haven, 1949), pp. 36 ff., asserts that this play "was acted by the children of the Queen's Revels on January 3, 1605; it had been entered on the Stationers' Register November 29, 1604, and was published . . . in 1605." He confesses that "the acting of the play is inferential." In fact, he simply assumed that, because the Queen's Revels acted at court on that date, they must have acted *Philotas!* It is most improbable that a play to which the Privy Council objected was ever put on at court. It is equally improbable that it was sold to a publisher by either author or actors *before* it was acted. Michel's edition prints Daniel's two letters of apology, one to Lord Mountjoy, Essex' friend and Penelope Devereaux' lover, now Earl of Devonshire, and the other to Robert Cecil, Viscount Cranbourne. He also prints Daniel's "Apology" although he did not find it in the 1605 edition. This edition was dedicated to Prince Henry, to whom Daniel laments having been "now mistaken by the censuring stage."

7. *Ben Jonson: Discoveries 1641; Conversations with William Drummond of Hawthornden 1619*, Bodley Head Quartos V, ed. G. B. Harrison (London, 1923), *Conversations*, p. 14. Also *Jonson*, IV, 329, and, on the danger of history plays being interpreted topically, I, 587–90. Arthur Wilson, *Life and Reign of James the First* (1653), p. 792, says of King James, "Some parallel'd him to *Tiberius* for Dissimulation, yet Peace was maintained by him." Tiberius is the Emperor in *Sejanus*. Wilson (1595–1652) was attached to the Devereaux Earls, and was a clerk in the exchequer office under King James.

8. *Sejanus*, like *Philotas*, was published in 1605, but it was not until it appeared in Jonson's *Works* in 1616 that it was described as "first acted in the yeere 1603. By the King's Maiesties Servants." It was not liked by the audience. One set of commendatory verses indicates that the popular rejection occurred at the Globe. Since the

public theaters were closed from the death of Queen Elizabeth until April, 1604, we must assume that this failure occurred either before the Queen died or after April, 1604. See ch. I, pp. 7–8 and nn. 20, 21; and see Chambers, *Elizabethan Stage,* III, 366–67. In Vol. II, pp. 210, Chambers suggests that *Sejanus* was "probably" one of the plays produced before the end of 1603 before King James. This seems impossible, if it failed on the public stage and was censured by the Privy Council. On the other hand, it can hardly be dated early in 1603, before the Queen died, since Northampton, whom Jonson blames for calling him before the Privy Council, was not added to that body until James came to England. *Sejanus* was entered in the Stationers' Register on November 2, 1604, by Edward Blount, who did not publish it, but transferred the title, on August 6, 1605, to Thomas Thorpe, who published it before the end of the year (Arber, III, 273, 297). Daniel's *Philotas* was also entered in November, 1604, by Simon Waterson (Daniel's usual publisher) and Edward Blount, but it also was not published until 1605.

9. He attributed the trouble over it to the malice of Northampton, who "was his mortall enemie for brailing on a St. George Day one of his attenders" (*Conversations,* p. 14).

10. Chambers, *Elizabethan Stage,* III, 254–56; *Jonson,* XI, 578, 585. Jonson's account of the affair, in *Conversations,* p. 12, is highly improbable. Just how could he "voluntarily imprison himself"? Does he mean that he surrendered to the authorities? He was in prison long enough to write to his most powerful acquaintances for help, and, according to his story, his mother was prepared to save him from mutilation by giving him poison. Chambers suggests that the imprisonment came after the publication of the play, in the autumn of 1605, rather than after the stage presentation, but in that case the publisher, rather than, or as well as, the author would have been in trouble. It seems probable that Jonson, long after the event, and somewhat fuddled with drink, confused the details of his several imprisonments, or that Drummond did.

11. *Othello* was probably first produced at the Globe in Michael-

mas Term, which began September 29, 1604. August 9 to 27 twelve of the King's Men, presumably including Shakespeare, were in attendance on the Spanish ambassador at Somerset House (Chambers, *Elizabethan Stage*, IV, 169–70). This was the occasion of the signing of the treaty of peace with Spain. A portrait of all the commissioners was painted, and everything was done to impress the Spaniards and solemnize the occasion. The attendance of the players suggests that there were plays, and this may have been the occasion on which the King saw *Much Ado*.

12. The King's Men went to Wilton, where the King was staying, on December 2, to put on a play which tradition makes *As You Like It* (Chambers, *Shakespeare*, II, 329; and *Elizabethan Stage*, IV, 117–18). They were also paid for plays put on on December 26, 27, 28, and 30, and two on January 1 (one a play of Robin Goodfellow), and on February 2 and 16.

13. Chambers, in *Elizabethan Stage*, IV, 139–40, and *Shakespeare*, II, 331–32, puts the performance "either at Southampton's house or Cranborne's" on the basis of a jocular remark in Cope's letter, and dates the performance "between 8 and 15 January." But Carleton's letter of January 15 makes it clear that "the corpus cum causa," i.e., the Queen, not the play, was entertained at both houses, at Southampton's first, and two days later at Lord Cranbourne's. Since it is reported in a letter dated the 15th, the latter cannot have been later than the 14th, nor Southampton's earlier than the 9th, since there was a play at court on the 8th.

14. Chambers, *Elizabethan Stage*, IV, 119.

15. Daniel was censor for the Queen's Revels, and his trouble over *Philotas* may have reduced the boys' repertory.

16. Jonson had been employed by the Spensers of Althorp to entertain the Queen with a mask on her way south from Scotland, June 25, 1603. He had written a part of the pageant for the King's long delayed Coronation procession, which took place March 15, 1604, and he promptly published his part, along with his "Panegyre"

to King James. He had also written an "entertainment" for the King when he was a guest of Sir William Cornwallis at his house in Highgate on May Day, 1604.

17. The text of the Folio bears the marks of early and experimental verse, with little evidence of patching.

18. Carleton's letter is quoted by Chambers (*Shakespeare,* II, 332).

19. Chambers, *Elizabethan Stage,* IV, 117–18.

20. See n. 18 above.

21. Queen Elizabeth was present at plays paid for by her courtiers (Chambers, *Stage,* I, 214, and n. 2). For plays provided by his hosts for King James, see *ibid.,* p. 215, n. 3.

22. *Much Ado about Nothing,* II, i, 110–35, 182–89, 215–34. I cite and quote The Pelican Shakespeare (Baltimore, Md., 1958).

23. Clifford Leech, "The Meaning of *Measure for Measure,"* *Shakespeare Survey,* III (1950), 73.

24. *The Shakespeare Allusion-Book,* Clement Mansfield Inglesby, *et al.,* ed. John Munro (London, 1932), I, 194. T. W. Baldwin, in *The Organization and Personnel of the Shakespearean Company* (Princeton, 1927), Plate III, before p. 229, casts Armin as Pompey and Cowley as Elbow, but Chambers challenges his premises. If, as Henslowe's diary and the court calender show, the same company put on several different plays in the same week, it seems that there must have been some more equitable distribution of labor than one which would, for example, give Burbage every leading part, or make Armin play Pompey because it is a bigger part than Elbow's.

25. John Dover Wilson, in the New Cambridge Edition (1962), discusses the revisions, pp. 98–135. Chambers, in *Shakespeare,* I, 331–38, discusses the revisions reflected in the Quarto of 1598. W. W. Greg, in *The Shakespeare First Folio* (Oxford, 1955), pp. 219–24, reviews the whole problem.

26. The sequence of these two plays is discussed by G. K. Hunter in his recent edition of *All's Well that Ends Well,* New Arden Edition (Cambridge, Mass., 1959), pp. xviii-xxv.

27. *Ibid.*, p. xxiv, n. 1.

28. See my article, "New Techniques of Comedy in *All's Well that Ends Well*," forthcoming in *Shakespeare Quarterly*, XVIII.

29. Hunter, in *All's Well that Ends Well*, New Arden Edition, pp. xv-xvi, cites, as evidence that Shakespeare sometimes composed with particular actors in mind, the Quartos of *Much Ado*, Act IV, scene ii; *Romeo and Juliet*, Act IV, scene v; *2 Henry IV*, Act V, scene iv, and the "E" and "G" (for Ecclestone and Gough), designating two lords or gentlemen in *All's Well*. Christopher Sly, in *The Taming of the Shrew* might be mentioned, and one or two other instances might be cited.

CHAPTER VIII. THE DUKE AS ACTOR AND PLAYWRIGHT

1. "Introduction" to the New Cambridge Edition, p. xiii.

2. *Survey*, p. 215. C. Leech also finds "something odd in the relations between the Duke and Lucio" ("The Meaning of *Measure for Measure*," *Shakespeare Survey* III [1950], 71).

3. "Introduction," p. xl.

4. Recently Bertram Evans has attempted to analyze the uses of multiple awareness in the comedies, in *Shakespeare's Comedies* (Oxford, 1960).

CHAPTER IX. SHAKESPEARE AS ACTOR

1. Reprinted in Chambers, *Shakespeare*, II, 264–69. Something of the quality of Rowe's information can be gathered from his assertion that Shakespeare "had three Daughters, of which two liv'd to be marry'd; *Judith*, the Elder," etc. On the other hand, if Shakespeare usually played a leading role, seeing him in a very minor one would cause surprised comment. The part of the Ghost could be doubled by the actor who played Claudius, and we know that doubling, as a way of providing actors for minor parts, was common.

2. Jonson, quoted in Chambers, *Shakespeare*, II, 207.

3. *Ibid.,* pp. 207–9.

4. Both Jonson and Digges were dead in 1640. Both were still alive in 1632 when the second Folio appeared. Digges's lines printed in the first Folio are in the same meter, but could never have been a part of this poem.

5. Chambers, *Shakespeare,* II, 232.

6. *Ibid.,* p. 210, from *Timber,* begun in 1623.

7. *Ibid.,* p. 230.

8. *Ibid.,* pp. 224–25. Beaumont died in 1616.

9. *Ibid.,* pp. 235.

10. *John Milton: Complete Poems and Major Prose,* ed. M. Y. Hughes (New York, 1957), p. 71.

11. E. K. Chambers, *Shakespeare,* II, 245.

12. *Ibid.,* p. 249.

13. *Ibid.,* p. 261; and see p. 262: "he wrote in a Charnel House in the midst of the Night."

14. *Ibid.,* I, 84. This story, first reported by William Oldys (*c.* 1743–61), is attributed to "one of Shakespeare's younger brothers," who lived until after the Restoration, when he was questioned by the actors! "There was besides a kinsman and descendant of the family, who was then a celebrated actor among them." This is apparently a conflation of Davenant and Betterton. Shakespeare's brothers all died before him, Edmund in 1607, Gilbert in 1612, and Richard in 1613.

15. *Shakespeare,* I, 84.

16. They are printed in Chambers, *Shakespeare,* II, 71–77. Chambers prints also the actor-lists for three plays of Beaumont and Fletcher, none of them earlier than 1611.

17. See above, Ch. VII, p. 4.

18. See Chambers, *Shakespeare,* I, 69–72. Karl J. Holzknecht, in *The Backgrounds of Shakespeare's Plays* (New York, 1950), p. 29, also discounts the story, as does T. M. Parrott, in *William Shakespeare: a Handbook* (New York, 1955), pp. 54–55.

19. *Shakespeare*, I, 84; and see II, 70, 249. Chambers makes a place for gossip and legend.

20. Reprinted in Chambers, *Shakespeare*, II, 188–89.

21. *Ibid.*, 189.

22. One of Aubrey's informers was William Beeston, son of Christopher Beeston, who acted in *Every Man in His Humour* in 1598, and is described as a servant of Augustine Philipps in 1605 (*ibid.*, II, 252–54).

23. Chambers, *Shakespeare*, II, 213–14.

24. Epigram 159, p. 76. Chambers, in *Shakespeare*, II, 213–14, comments that the "bit about 'companion for a King' is cryptic," and speculates about a possible meaning.

25. *Basilikon Doron*, p. 127.

26. See Chambers, *Shakespeare*, I, 79.

27. *Ibid.*, II, 73.

28. *Ibid.*, II, 70: "Shakespeare not improbably gave up acting at an early date," which rather extends forward Rowe's account of his retirement in "the latter part of his life," to Stratford, and John Ward's statement that "in his elder days [he] lived at Stratford" (see II, 249).

29. *Microcosmos*, 215, and Chambers, *Shakespeare*, II, 213.

30. *Ibid.*, II, 214; Davies, *The Civile Warres of Death and Fortune* (1605), p. 183.

31. Chambers, *Shakespeare*, II, 212.

32. See, for example, Una Ellis-Fermor, *Shakespeare the Dramatist* (New York, 1961), pp. 16–18. She speaks of his "limitless sympathy," and his capacity for "wholly imagined . . . character."

CHAPTER X: CONCLUSIONS

1. Leslie Hotson's attempt to recreate *The First Night of "Twelfth Night"* is concerned with the audience, and his theory that the play presented on this occasion was *Twelfth Night*, even if we accept it, throws very little light on the play itself.

2. Those who are shocked by Isabella's desertion of her intent to become a nun (a "bride of Christ") might consider the archetypal implication of her tacit acceptance of the Duke's proposal.

3. The Arden Shakespeare (London, 1962), pp. xxiii–xxiv.

4. *Ibid.*, p. xxiv.

Index

Both text and notes are included. Where a short reference is encountered in the notes, the full reference can be found by looking up the author in the index. Although subject entries are as complete for the notes as for the text, proper names and short references in the notes are usually omitted, while proper names in the text are indexed. Names of characters in plays other than *Measure for Measure* are followed by the title of the play in parentheses, except for Hamlet, Henry V, and Othello. Titles of works other than Shakespeare's are followed by the name of the author in parentheses. Works are listed under the name of the author except for Shakespeare's works, which are indexed by title, and works referred to in the text by title.

200